THE ART OF CASH FLOW

Navigating the Path to Financial Success

CA. RV. Saurabh Agrawal

ISBN 979-8-89067-654-2

CONTENTS

ABOUT THE AUTHOR

Saurabh Agrawal is a highly accomplished professional, holding the prestigious designation of **Fellow Chartered Accountant** and **Registered Valuer** under class Securities and Financial Assets. With over 12 years of extensive experience, he is a seasoned practitioner in providing a wide range of services, including consulting, audit, accounting, and taxation. Throughout his career, Saurabh has been dedicated to serving various industries as a trusted consultant.

Saurabh Agrawal has also built a stellar reputation in the field of valuation. With his expertise as a Registered Valuer, he has successfully conducted valuations for numerous prominent companies across various industries.

His passion for continuous learning is evident through his impressive list of certifications, including a diploma in ISA (Information Systems Audit), a certificate course on valuation by ICAI (Institute of Chartered Accountants of India), a Certification Course on Concurrent Audits of Banks, and a Certificate Course on Forensic Accounting and Fraud Detection. These certifications showcase his expertise in multiple facets of the financial domain.

His proficiency in business valuation has led him to handle assignments for well-known companies, earning him recognition for delivering accurate and comprehensive valuation reports. Through meticulous analysis and in-depth understanding of market dynamics, Saurabh has provided invaluable insights to business owners, investors, and stakeholders, helping them make informed decisions with confidence.

Saurabh Agrawal's contributions to the field of indirect taxation are commendable, with his valuable insights shared through numerous articles and lectures. He has authored the well-regarded "GST PRACTICE MANUAL AND READY REFERENCE," which has become a go-to resource for those seeking clarity in the complex realm of indirect taxation.

With an impressive track record of successful valuations for many companies, Saurabh Agrawal brings a wealth of experience to the table. His expertise in both financial advisory and valuation domains makes him a well-rounded professional, capable of offering comprehensive financial solutions to businesses of all scales.

AUTHOR'S NOTE

Greetings to all business owners and aspiring entrepreneurs,

I am absolutely thrilled to present you with my book, "The Art of Cash Flow: Navigating the path to Financial Success." This book is all about helping you understand the critical aspect of managing money in your business. Throughout my extensive career spanning 12 years as a consultant, I have had the privilege of working with a diverse range of clients, witnessing their triumphs and challenges in the dynamic world of business.

One thing that caught my attention during my interactions with business owners is the common challenge of financial management. Many entrepreneurs possess great expertise in their products or services but tend to overlook the significance of handling money effectively. This oversight can lead to persistent cash flow problems and missed opportunities for growth. I firmly believe that financial management should be a strategic process, not an ongoing worry.

Through the pages of this book, my ultimate goal is to emphasize the importance of closely monitoring your cash flow. I want to assure you that understanding and managing your finances is not as complicated as it may seem. I have taken special care to explain the concepts in simple and accessible language, making it easy for anyone, regardless of their financial background, to prepare a cash flow statement and monitor their business's cash flows effectively.

In my extensive experience, I have observed two distinct types of business owners – those who skilled in financial management and those who struggle with it. The former group always seems to be in control, making informed decisions with a clear understanding of their financial position. On the other hand, the latter group often finds themselves overwhelmed and constantly worried about managing their business.

With this book, I aspire to inspire all business owners, especially those running small and medium-sized enterprises, to never lose sight of their company's financial health, with a keen focus on cash flows. I want to empower you with the knowledge and tools needed to master your business's cash flow. I firmly believe that a well-managed cash flow can help you tackle financial challenges proactively and ensure your business remains in excellent financial condition. Cash flow statement," a powerful tool that allows you to categorize your cash flows and identify actionable insights. By adopting this approach, you can confidently address financial challenges and make informed decisions for the growth and success of your business.

As we embark on this exciting journey together, I want you to feel in control of your finances and confident in achieving financial success. I am deeply committed to supporting you through this book, as well as through the quality services I offer.

Thank you for joining me in this exploration of financial management. I wish you the very best of luck in your entrepreneurial endeavors.

Sincerely,

Saurabh Agrawal

CASH DYNAMICS

A Puzzle For Entrepreneurs

Before starting the book, I want to tell you one thing that there is a big difference between "knowing how to swim" and "Really Swim". Similarly, "running or managing a business" is entirely different "from that small business through which you fulfill your dreams and achieving your vision which you see when you started". Therefore, if you want to become an expert in business, Sahab! Motivation alone is not enough. What you need practically, the most necessary thing for you is funds.

Money! Yes, that's right. Money, the lifeblood of any business, can sometimes feel like it's playing hide-and-seek with us, just out of reach when we need it the most. It's the fuel that keeps the engine running smoothly and enables us to turn our dreams into reality. From the very first day of starting a business, funds is an absolute necessity. Without sufficient funds, Our grand visions and ambitious plans remain unrealized dreams, forever trapped in the realm of fantasy, unable to manifest in the tangible world.

Imagine you've developed a groundbreaking product that has the potential to revolutionize an industry. But here's the catch – you have no funds to produce inventory, market your product, reach customers, and fulfill orders. Without cash, your brilliant product remains stuck on the drawing board.

But here's the thing - the importance of funds or cash doesn't end with the initial stages of our business. Even well-established enterprises require a steady flow of funds to maintain their operations, support expansion endeavors, and seize opportunities in the ever-changing market landscape. Money becomes the life force that drives our research and development efforts, fuels our marketing initiatives, attracts top-notch talent, and ensures efficient inventory management. Without a solid financial foundation, businesses can find themselves struggling to meet their obligations, hindering their growth potential and putting their long-term viability at risk.

The cash is a relatable experience that many of us encounter. It's like holding sand in our hands, no matter how tightly we grip it, some of it always seems to slip away. We can observe this phenomenon in our personal lives and even in the world of business.

Consider a situation where you receive your paycheck at the end of the month. On paper, it looks like a substantial amount, but as the days go by, you find that the money diminishes rapidly. You pay your bills, cover necessary expenses, and suddenly, You're left perplexed, wondering where it all went.

Similarly, in the business world, entrepreneurs often encounter this enigma. They work tirelessly, focusing on growing their revenue and maximizing their profits. However, when they look at their financial statements, they're surprised to find that despite the healthy profits shown, their cash flow remains elusive.

Let's consider an example to illustrate this situation. Imagine a small retail business that experiences a surge in sales,

Customers rush to the store, and the business generates substantial revenue and profits. However, as the owner closely monitors the cash flow, they realize that the money from these sales doesn't immediately translate into cash.

Why does this happen? Well, in the case of the retail business, there are several factors. Firstly, customers may make purchases on credit, deferring the actual cash inflow. Secondly, the business must manage its inventory and procure new stock to meet customer demand, which requires cash outflows. Additionally, there may be expenses such as rent, utilities, and employee salaries that need to be paid promptly.

Have you ever witnessed businesses that appeared to be thriving suddenly crumble and go bankrupt? To understand this concept better, let's look at an example. Imagine a family-owned restaurant that has been a local favorite for many years. The establishment has a loyal customer base, consistently high ratings, and seemingly healthy profits.

However, behind the scenes, the restaurant's owners have been neglecting key aspects of their operations. Over time, they failed to adapt to changing customer preferences and upgrade the dining experience, and became unworried with their menu offerings. Customers began to notice outdated offerings. Gradually, their loyal customer base started dwindling, leading to a decline in sales. They slowly deteriorate their financial health by neglecting the very thing they need most – "cash flow" By the time the owners realized the severity of the situation, it was too late. The poison of complacency and resistance to change had already taken its toll, ultimately leading to the downfall of the once-thriving restaurant.

One of the biggest problems lies in the lack of awareness and willingness to confront the issue. Many business owners believe that they know their company the best, having built it from the ground up. It's similar to a good father who possesses a deep understanding of his child. No one else can replace a father's role in a child's life. However, imagine a father who remains ignorant to certain needs of his child or focuses solely on one aspect while neglecting others. This one-sided approach can have disastrous consequences for the child's overall well-being and development.

In this case, can we truly consider the father as a good father? Despite his commitment to providing for his child, his ignorance of other crucial aspects hampers the child's overall well-being and development. A good father understands the diverse needs of their child and tries to balance and address them holistically.

Similarly, entrepreneurs who claim to know their companies inside out should recognize that effective business management requires a well-rounded approach. Just like the father who needs to consider all aspects of their child's well-being, entrepreneurs must acknowledge that running a successful company goes beyond focusing solely on one area, such as sales or profits, ignoring the warning signs of a cash flow crisis.

So, how can you do this? Many businesses fall into trouble simply because they fail to monitor things in a timely manner and operate on assumptions rather than facts. Business owners cannot escape the responsibility of managing their company's finances. Even in unfavorable external circumstances, they must take charge. There is no way around it. You must know how to capture this cash and how to monitor cash flow. They are focusing solely on their profit and loss accounts and balance sheet while neglecting the most important financial statement of all - the cash flow statement.

The cash flow statement is like a window into the heart of our business. It reveals the inflows and outflows of cash, providing valuable insights into the areas that need immediate attention and action. By analyzing this statement, we gain a deeper understanding of our liquidity challenges and can take proactive steps to address them.

But why is cash flow so important? Well, another crucial aspect is business valuation. When it comes to valuing a business, most famous and internationally accepted valuation method is the Discounted Cash Flow (DCF) Method. This method calculates the present value of projected future cash flows. If our business generates strong and consistent cash flows, it naturally leads to a higher valuation compared to a business with weaker cash flow prospects. It's a clear indication that monitoring our cash flow isn't just essential for day-to-day operations but also for the overall value and worth of our businesses.

By recognizing the importance of cash flow, monitoring closely, and taking proactive steps to manage and improve our cash position, we can break free from the cycle of liquidity challenges. Our businesses deserve financial stability, prosperity, and the opportunity to thrive in a competitive marketplace.

So, let's roll up our sleeves, dive into the depths of our cash flow statements, and capture that ever elusive cash once and for all.

PREQUEL OF CASH FLOW

02

Understand the Financial Statement

"You have to understand accounting and you have to understand the nuances of accounting. It's the language of business, and it's an imperfect language, but unless you are willing to put in the effort to learn accounting - how to read and interpret financial statements - you really shouldn't be in the business at all." - Warren Buffett

But as per my view "Accounting is the art of transforming complex financial data into concise and meaningful statements that speak the truth about a company's financial standing".

The first steps before understanding cash flow, looking at two important financial statements: the Profit and loss statement and the balance sheet.

- The Profit and loss statement tells us how much money a company made and how much it spent during a certain period. It shows the revenue earned (money coming in) and the expenses incurred (money going out) over that period.

- The balance sheet gives us a snapshot of the company's financial situation at a specific moment. It shows what the company owns (assets), what it owes (liabilities), and the portion of the company that belongs to the owners (shareholders' equity).

By looking at these statements, we can lay the groundwork for understanding cash flow. You can look at financial statements from two perspectives:

- as the person creating them (Accountants, book keepers etc.)
- as the person using them. (business owner, investor etc.)

The Accountants/book keepers creating the financial statements usually have a background in accounting. They work with ledger entries, bills, and receipts to track the flow of money in and out of the company. Their goal is to create transparent financial statements that accurately show the company's financial situation. This requires skills gained through training such as a articleship under Chartered Accountant.

On the other hand, the person using the financial statements like business owners, simply wants to understand them. They don't need to know every little detail about journal entries or audits. They just want to make sense of the statements so they can make decisions about the company

It's a common misconception that a business owners needs to know how to create financial statements in detail. While it's not always necessary to have that understanding. you only need to know how to use financial statements to make decisions. Creating them is not a requirement.

Because I have written this book with a focus on business owners, we will look at financial statements from their perspective only. We will understand financial statements in simple language, keeping the business owner's viewpoint in mind.

2.1   Profit and loss statement (P&L)

The prequel to cash flow starts with the preparation of Profit and Loss Statement, also known as the Income Statement, Statement of Operations, or Statement of Earnings, shows the financial transactions that occurred during a specific period. It provides information about:

- Revenue earned by the company during a set timeframe (annually or quarterly).
- Expenses incurred to generate that revenue.
- Depreciation and amortization expenses.
- Taxes
- Earnings per share of the company.

as per my experience, the best way to understand a financial statement is to look at the actual statement and try to grasp the information provided. We are taking M/s Infosys Limited annual report for our understanding. Statement of profit and loss account of M/s Infosys limited as follows:

Statement of Profit and Loss		(In ₹ crore)	
Particular	Note	Year ended march 31,	
		2023	2022
Revenue from operation	2.18	124014	103940
Other Income, net	2.19	3859	3224
Total Income		127873	107164
Expenses			
Employee benefit expenses	2.2	62764	51664
Cost of technical sub-contractors		19096	16298
Travel expenses		1227	731
Cost of software packages and others	2.2	5214	2985
Communication expenses		502	433

Contd...

Statement of Profit and Loss			(In ₹ crore)
Particular	Note	Year ended march 31,	
Consultancy and professional charges		1236	1511
Depreciation and amortization expenses	2.1, 2.2.2 and 2.3	2753	2429
Finance cost	2.3	157	128
Other expenses	2.2	3281	2490
Total expenses		96230	78669
Profit before tax		31643	28495
Tax expense:			
Current tax	2.17	8167	6960
Deferred tax	2.17	208	300
Profit for the year		23268	21235

2.1.1 Some basic points

- The P&L statement is for the year ending on March 31, 2023. This means it is an annual statement for that particular year, not a quarterly statement. Also, if this statement is for March 31, 2023, it represents the financial year 2022-23 or FY23.
- All the numbers provided here are in Crore rupees. Please note that 1 crore is equal to 100 lakh rupees. It entirely depends on the company to decide in which unit they want to present the numbers in the statement.
- The statement provides a detailed breakdown of all the key items, and any related notes or schedules are given in the note section. Each note has a specific note number assigned to it.
- Traditionally, companies present the current year's number in the left column and the previous

year's number in the right column in their financial statements. In this example, FY23 number is in the left column and FY22 number is in the right column.

2.1.2 Revenue

You may have often heard experts talk about a *company's top line*. In reality, they are referring to the revenue mentioned in the P&L statement. When a company presents its P&L statement, it starts by disclosing the revenue or income.

As you can see in the above Profit and loss statement of M/S Infosys Limited, they have break the total revenue in 2-3 points as follows:

- The main income derived from the company's core operations is called "Revenue from Operations. Here Infosys main object is software services so any revenue come from there is fall under this category. If you look in note 2.18 this figure is 1,23,755 Crores.
- Any other income related to the primary business is classified under "Other Operating Income." Here Infosys main object is software services but many time to fulfill that main object we have to provide other services with main services therefore any revenue come from this particular service is fall under this category. If you look in note 2.18 this figure is 259 crores. Total of both point become revenue from operations.

Note: 2.18	(in ₹ crore)	
Particular	Year ended march 31,	
	2023	2022
Revenue from software services	1,23,755	1,03,615
Revenue from products and platforms	259	325
Total revenue from operations	1,24,014	1,03,940

Income from any other source is categorized as "Other income." In our example Infosys have many line items of other income like Interest income on financial assets, Income on investments, Dividend received from subsidiary, Exchange gains / (losses) on foreign currency etc.

2.1.3   Expenses

In a company, the expenses related to various activities are divided into different categories. This division is usually done based on the nature of the expenses or by using the cost of sales method. It helps the company keep track of where their money is being spent. Here we can see many line items in Infosys P&L like Employee benefit expenses, Cost of technical sub-contractors, Travel expenses, Cost of software packages, Communication expenses, Consultancy and professional charges, Finance Cost etc. in P&L, last line item of expenses is Other expenses, this is total of many other small expenses which is not required to know in detail by giving them separate line item.

It is important for every expense of the company to be recorded either in the profit and loss statement or in the notes section. These financial documents provide a clear picture of the company's financial health and help stakeholders understand how money is being used.

If you look closely at the expenses listed, you will notice that each expense has a note attached to it. These notes serve a significant purpose. They provide additional details and explanations about the specific expense, giving a deeper understanding of why and how the money was spent. These notes are valuable for investors, auditors, and anyone analyzing the company's financial statements. They offer transparency and clarity, ensuring that all expenses are properly accounted for and can be thoroughly examined.

By categorizing and documenting expenses in this way, companies can effectively manage their finances, make informed decisions, and demonstrate financial accountability to stakeholders.

2.1.4 Depreciation and Amortization Expenses

Depreciation and amortization are important expenses for a company. In this case, the company spent 2,753 crore rupees on these expenses. To understand this better, we need to know about tangible and intangible assets.

Tangible assets are physical assets that have a visible presence and can be included in the company's total assets. Examples include laptops, cars, machinery, buildings, and factories. On the other hand, intangible assets lack physical existence but possess value that can be accounted for, such as trademarks, copyrights, patents, and brand value.

The special thing about any asset is that it depreciates over time as its useful life. Each asset has a specific useful life. For example, the useful life of a laptop could be 3 years. The useful life of an asset is the period until it remains valuable for the company. Let's understand this with an example.

A stock brokerage firm named Choice International earned a total income of ₹10,00,000. However, during this period, the company spent ₹6,50,000 to purchase a large computer server. The useful life of this computer server is considered to be 5 years. Now, if you look at Choice International's figures, you will see that the company earned ₹10,00,000 but spent ₹6,50,000. So, the company only made a profit of ₹3,50,000, right? But these figures don't give us the complete picture.

Remember that this asset (the computer server) was purchased this year but its useful life extends to the next 5 years. Therefore, it is important to allocate its cost over the next 5 years rather than showing it as a one-time large expense. This way, ₹6,50,000 will be allocated over 5 years, which means ₹1,30,000 will be depreciated each year. After showing this depreciation, Choice International's earnings will be ₹10,00,000 - ₹1,30,000 = ₹8,70,000.

Similarly, the value of intangible assets is also considered, but instead of depreciation, it is referred to as amortization.

Now, there is an important thing to understand here. Choice International depreciated its server for a period of 5 years and allocated the cost over 5 years. But in reality, the company spent ₹65,000. Now, where will this expense be shown in the P&L statement? As a business owner, how will we know where the company's money went? For this, we need to look at the cash flow statement. We will discuss this further in the upcoming chapters.

2.1.5 Taxes

In simple terms, when we deduct all expenses from revenue, but taxes are still pending, we refer to the remaining profit as "Profit Before Tax" or PBT. Looking at the provided P&L statement of Infosys, Profit before taxes is 31,643 Crore Rupees.

we need to subtract all types of tax expenses from the Profit Before Tax (PBT). Here, "current tax" refers to the corporate tax payable for the current year, which amounts to 8,167 Crores. Additionally, the company has mentioned other taxes as well. Combining all the taxes, the company has paid a total of 8,375 Crores in taxes.

After deducting taxes from the total earnings of the company, the remaining amount is called the "Operating Profit" or " Profit After Tax" (PAT). It is also referred to as the "bottom line" of the P&L. If we subtract the tax amount of 8,375 Crores from the PBT of 31,643 Crores, we arrive at the PAT of 23,268 Crores.

2.1.6 Earnings per share

The last section of a P&L statement includes EPS (Earnings Per Share), which is presented in both diluted and basic forms. EPS is widely used for financial analysis of a company. By looking at EPS, we can understand how effectively the company's directors and managers are running the company. EPS is a measure that indicates how much profit, the management of the company has generated on each share. It provides insights into the company's profitability and helps investors evaluate the company's performance. By calculating EPS, we can assess the financial health of the company and make informed decisions about investing in its shares.

In simple terms, EPS tells us how much money the company has earned per share. It is a key metric for understanding a company's earnings and is widely used in financial analysis.

2.2 Balance sheet

Unlike the P&L statement, which focuses on the company's profitability for a specific period, the balance sheet provides a historical overview of the company's financial growth and stability. By analyzing the balance sheet, investors and stakeholders can assess the company's liquidity, solvency, and overall financial stability. It helps in evaluating the company's ability to meet its short-term and long-term obligations, the value of its assets, and the portion of the company owned by shareholders. The balance sheet provides a snapshot of the company's financial position at a specific point in time. It provides information about:

- Shareholders' fund
- Non-current Liabilities
- Current Liabilities
- Non-current Assets
- Current Assets

For deep understanding, We will divide balance sheet into side as follows:

- **Assets Side of balance sheet,** This side shows us all the company's assets right from its inception. the Asset side has two main sections, i.e. Non-current assets and Current assets.
- **Liability Side of Balance sheet,** this side of the balance sheet details all the liabilities of the company. Within liabilities, there are three

sub-sections – shareholders' fund, non-current liabilities, and current liabilities.

2.2.1 The Assets Side of balance sheet

An asset owned by a company is expected to give the company an economic benefit over its useful life. In simple terms are the resources held by a company, which help in generating the revenues. Here is the snapshot of the Assets side of the balance sheet:

Balance Sheet			(In ₹ crore)
Particulars	Note	As at March 31,	
		2023	2022
Assets			
Non Current Assets			
Property, plant and equipment	2.1	11656	11384
Right-of-use assets	2.3	3561	3311
Capital work-in-progress	2.4	275	411
Good will	2.2	211	211
Other intangible assets	2.2	3	32
Financial assets			
Investments	2.5	23686	22869
Loans	2.6	39	34
Other financial assets	2.7	1341	727
Deferred tax assets (net)	2.17	779	970
Income tax assets (net)	2.17	5916	5585
Other non-current assets	2.1	1788	1416
Total non-current assets		**49255**	**46950**
Current assets			
Financial assets			
Investments	2.5	4476	5467
Trade receivables	2.8	20773	18966

Contd…

Balance Sheet			(In ₹ crore)
Cash and cash equivalents	2.9	6534	12270
Loans	2.6	291	219
Other financial assets	2.7	9088	6580
Other current assets	2.1	10920	8935
Total current assets		**52082**	**52437**
Total assets		**101337**	**99387**

As you can see, the Asset side has two main sections, i.e. Non-current assets and Current assets.

2.2.1.1 **Non-Current Assets**

Non-current assets, also known as long-term assets, are a significant component of a company's balance sheet. They represent assets that are expected to provide economic benefits to the company for more than one accounting period, typically longer than a year. These assets are not intended for immediate sale or conversion into cash but rather play a vital role in the company's long-term operations and growth.

Non-current assets can be categorized into different subcategories based on their nature and characteristics. Some common types of non-current assets include:

- ***Property, Plant, and Equipment (PP&E)***: This category includes tangible assets such as land, buildings, machinery, equipment, vehicles, and furniture. Tangible fixed assets are essential for a company's daily operations and contribute to its production or service delivery. They are typically recorded at their historical cost and are subject to depreciation over their useful lives.

- *Intangible Assets:* Intangible assets lack physical substance but hold value for the company. They include assets such as patents, trademarks, copyrights, brand names, customer lists, proprietary technology, and goodwill. Intangible assets contribute to a company's competitive advantage and are often recorded at their fair value or cost and amortized over their useful lives.
- *Investments:* Non-current investments refer to long-term investments made by the company in other entities, such as equity securities, bonds, or long-term loans to other companies. These investments are not intended for immediate liquidation but rather for generating income or strategic purposes.
- *Long-term Financial Assets:* These include long-term loans or receivables, such as loans provided to customers or business partners with repayment terms extending beyond one year.
- *Deferred Charges*: Deferred charges are costs that are capitalized and amortized over their useful life. They typically include prepaid expenses or costs related to long-term contracts or lease agreements.
- *Non-current assets*: Prepaid expenses that are expected to benefit the company beyond the next operating cycle are classified as non-current assets. Examples include prepaid insurance premiums, long-term leases, or prepaid royalties.

Non-current assets are important for assessing a company's financial health, growth potential, and ability to generate future cash flows. They reflect the company's long-term investment in resources that support its operations and contribute to its value. Stakeholders, including investors, lenders, and analysts, closely analyze non-current assets to understand a company's asset base, its utilization, and its potential for generating returns in the future. It's important to note that the valuation and disclosure of non-current assets are subject to accounting standards and regulations to ensure transparency and comparability across companies.

2.2.1.2   Current Assets

Current assets are a key component of a company's balance sheet and represent assets that are expected to be converted into cash or used up within a short period, typically within one year. These assets are essential for day-to-day operations and the ongoing business cycle. Let's explore some common categories of current assets:

- *Cash and Cash Equivalents*: This includes physical currency, bank account balances, and highly liquid investments that can be readily converted into cash. Cash equivalents are short-term investments with maturities of three months or less.
- *Accounts Receivable*: These are amounts owed to the company by customers or clients for goods or services provided on credit. Accounts receivable represent the company's right to receive payment and are usually collected within a short timeframe.
- *Inventory*: Inventory comprises goods held by a company for sale or production. It includes raw materials, work-in-progress, and finished goods. Inventory is valued at the lower of cost or net realizable value and represents assets that are

expected to be sold within the normal course of business.

- *Prepaid Expenses*: Prepaid expenses are costs paid in advance for goods or services that will be consumed or utilized in the future. Examples include prepaid insurance premiums, prepaid rent, or prepaid subscriptions.
- *Short-term Investments*: These are investments that are readily marketable and have maturities of more than three months but less than one year. Short-term investments may include treasury bills, commercial paper, or money market funds.
- *Other Current Assets*: This category encompasses various assets that don't fall into the above categories but are expected to be converted into cash within one year. It may include items such as advances to suppliers, deposits, or accrued income.

Current assets play a crucial role in a company's liquidity and ability to meet short-term obligations. They provide a snapshot of a company's operational efficiency, cash flow management, and overall financial health. By analyzing the composition and trends of current assets, investors and stakeholders can gain insights into the company's ability to generate cash, manage working capital, and support ongoing business activities.

2.2.2   The Liability Side of Balance sheet

The liabilities side of the balance sheet details all the liabilities of the company. Within liabilities, there are three sub-sections – shareholders' fund, non-current liabilities, and current liabilities.

Balance Sheet (contd.)

Particulars	Note	As at March 31, 2023	As at March 31, 2022
		2023	2022
Equity and liability			
Equity			
Equity share capital	2.12	2074	2103
Other equity		65671	67203
Total equity		**67745**	**69306**
Liabilities			
Non-current liabilities			
Financial liabilities			
Lease liabilities	2.3	3553	3228
Other financial liabilities	2.13	1317	676
Deferred tax liabilities (net)	2.17	866	841
Other non-current liabilities	2.15	414	360
Total non-current liabilities		**6150**	**5105**
Current liabilities			
Financial liabilities			
Lease liabilities	2.3	713	558
Trade payables	2.14		
Total outstanding dues of enterprises and small enterprises		97	3
Total outstanding dues of creditors other than micro enterprises and small enterprises		2329	2666
Other financial liabilities	2.13	12697	11269
Other current liabilities	2.15	7609	7381
Provisions	2.16	1163	920
Income tax liabilities (net)	2.17	2834	2179
Total current liabilities		**27442**	**24976**
Total equity and liabilities		**101337**	**99387**

The accompanying form an integral part of the Standalone financial statements.

2.2.2.1 Share holders' fund

The shareholders' fund, which is integral to the balance sheet's liabilities side, is highlighted in the snapshot below. Many people find this term a little confusing. if you think about it, we are discussing liabilities that represent the company's obligation. On the other hand, we discuss the shareholders' fund, which represents the shareholders' wealth. This is quite counter-intuitive, isn't it? How can liabilities and shareholders' funds appear on the 'Liabilities' side of the balance sheet?

To gain a better understanding, let's consider the company as an individual who is responsible for operating the business and generating wealth for its shareholders. This also means the shareholders' funds do not belong to the company as it rightfully belongs to its shareholders'. Therefore, from the company's perspective, the shareholders' funds are considered an obligation or liability that needs to be paid back to the shareholders. Hence this is shown on the liabilities side of the balance sheet.

Shareholders' funds comprise several components that represent the financial contributions and accumulated earnings of the company's shareholders. These components include:

- *Share Capital*: Share capital represents the total value of shares issued by the company to its shareholders. It reflects the initial investment made by shareholders in exchange for ownership rights and represents their ownership stake in the company.

- *Share Premium*: Share premium refers to the additional amount received by the company when issuing shares above their nominal value. It represents the premium paid by investors for acquiring shares and is recorded as a reserve on the balance sheet.
- *Retained Earnings*: Retained earnings are the accumulated profits earned by the company that have not been distributed to shareholders as dividends. These earnings are reinvested back into the business for future growth, research and development, debt repayment, or other business purposes.
- *Other Reserves*: Other reserves include various funds set aside by the company, such as capital reserves, revaluation reserves, and general reserves. Capital reserves may arise from specific transactions, such as the sale of assets or share premium cancellation. Revaluation reserves arise from the upward revaluation of assets, such as property or investments. General reserves are typically created to strengthen the company's financial position or address specific contingencies.

These components collectively form the shareholders' funds, representing the financial resources available to the company that are attributable to its shareholders. The shareholders' funds play a vital role in supporting the company's operations, expansion, and ability to generate returns for its shareholders. They serve as a measure of the company's net worth and represent the shareholders' claims on the company's assets in the event of liquidation.

2.2.2.2 Non-Current Liabilities

Non-current liabilities, also known as long-term liabilities, are financial obligations that extend beyond one year and are not expected to be settled in the near term. These liabilities represent the long-term financial obligations of the company. Here are some common examples of non-current liabilities:

- *Long-Term Loans*: Non-current liabilities may include long-term loans or bonds that the company has issued and is required to repay over an extended period, usually with interest. These loans are typically used for financing long-term investments, such as acquiring assets or funding expansion projects.
- *Deferred Tax Liabilities*: Deferred tax liabilities arise due to the discrepancy in the way the depreciation is treated. Deferred tax liabilities are amounts of income taxes payable in the future concerning taxable differences as per accounting books and tax books.
- *Pension Obligations*: If a company offers pension plans or other employee benefit plans, the associated obligations are classified as non-current liabilities. These liabilities represent the company's long-term commitment to provide retirement benefits to its employees.
- *Lease Obligations*: Non-current liabilities may also include lease obligations for long-term leases, such as lease agreements for office space, equipment, or vehicles. The company is required to make periodic lease payments over an extended period.

- *Deferred Revenue*: Deferred revenue represents payments received by a company in advance for goods or services that have not yet been delivered or rendered. These advance payments create a liability that is recognized as revenue over time as the goods are delivered or services are provided.

Non-current liabilities are essential for investors and creditors as they provide insights into the company's long-term financial obligations and its ability to meet those obligations. They are typically paid off over an extended period and may have an impact on the company's cash flow, profitability, and overall financial health. Monitoring non-current liabilities is crucial for assessing the company's long-term solvency and financial stability.

2.2.2.3 Non-Current Liabilities

Current liabilities are the financial obligations of a company that are expected to be settled within a short period, usually within one year or the operating cycle of the business. These are the liabilities that the company needs to pay off in the near future. Current liabilities are listed on the liabilities side of the balance sheet and include the following:

- *Accounts Payable*: Accounts payable represents the money owed by a company to its suppliers or vendors for goods or services that have been received but not yet paid for. It includes outstanding bills, invoices, or any other amounts that the company owes to its creditors.
- *Short-Term Loans*: Short-term loans are borrowings that need to be repaid within a year. These loans are often taken by businesses

to meet their short-term funding needs, such as managing cash flow or financing working capital requirements.

- *Accrued Expenses*: Accrued expenses are expenses that have been incurred but not yet paid. These can include salaries and wages owed to employees, interest payable on loans, taxes payable, or any other expenses that have been recorded but not settled.
- *Bank Overdraft*: A bank overdraft occurs when a company withdraws more money from its bank account than it has available. It creates a temporary negative balance in the account, and the company is required to repay the overdraft amount to the bank.
- *Unearned Revenue*: Unearned revenue, also known as deferred revenue or advance payments, represents the money received by a company in advance for goods or services that have not yet been provided. The company has an obligation to deliver the goods or services, and the unearned revenue is recognized as revenue over time as the obligations are fulfilled.

Current liabilities are important to monitor as they represent the company's short-term financial obligations and its ability to meet its immediate payment obligations. Managing current liabilities effectively is crucial for maintaining liquidity, cash flow stability, and ensuring the smooth operation of the business. By keeping track of current liabilities, companies can ensure they have enough funds to cover their short-term expenses and maintain a healthy financial position.

2.3   Relation between profit and loss account and balance sheet

To begin with, consider the **Revenue from Sales**. When a company makes a sale, it incurs expenses. For example, if the company undertakes an advertisement campaign to spread awareness about its products, the company has to **spend cash** on the campaign. The money spent tends to decrease the cash balance. If the company makes a sale on credit, the **Receivables** (Accounts Receivables) go higher.

we will now understand how the P&L and Balance Sheet line items are connected, Balance sheet and P&L statement are inseparable. They are connected in many ways. Have a look at the following image for more examples:

Connecting the P&L and Balance Sheet		
The P&L Statement		**The Balance Sheet statement**
Sales Revenue	➤➤➤	Receivables and Cash Balance
Operating Expenses	➤➤➤	Inventory and Trade Payables
Depreciation & Amortization	➤➤➤	Accumulated Depriciation
Other Income	➤➤➤	Investments
Finance Cost	➤➤➤	Debt
PAT	➤➤➤	Shareholders Equity

The prequel to cash flow starts with the preparation of the income statement (also known as the profit and loss statement) and the balance sheet. The income statement shows the revenues earned and expenses incurred during a specific period, while the balance sheet presents the company's assets, liabilities, and shareholders' equity at a particular point in time.

From these financial statements, we can determine the net income or net loss of the business. Net income is calculated by subtracting total expenses from total revenues. Net loss occurs when total expenses exceed total revenues.

The net income or net loss is an important starting point in understanding the prequel of cash flow. However, it's important to note that net income does not provide a complete picture of a company's cash position. It includes non-cash items such as depreciation and amortization, which are expenses that do not involve actual cash outflows.

To obtain a more accurate representation of a company's cash flows, we need to make adjustments for these non-cash items and consider changes in working capital. Working capital includes the company's current assets (such as cash, accounts receivable, and inventory) and current liabilities (such as accounts payable and accrued expenses).

By analyzing changes in working capital accounts and adjusting for non-cash expenses, we can determine the operating cash flow of the business. Operating cash flow represents the cash generated or used by the company's core operations.

The prequel of cash flow, therefore, involves understanding the net income or net loss from the income statement, making adjustments for non-cash items, and analyzing changes in working capital to arrive at the operating cash flow. This lays the foundation for further analysis of the cash flow statement, which provides a comprehensive view of a company's cash inflows and outflows during a given period.

BASICS OF CASH FLOW

03

Before we dive into the cash flow statement, let's take a step back and make sure we understand something crucial. You see, to truly grasp the cash flow statement, we need to first get a handle on a fundamental concept – and that's all about the activities of a company.

Think about any company you know, like your favorite local store or a popular tech company. Now, what do these companies actually do? Well, they engage in various business activities to run their operations smoothly. These activities can be divided into three main categories, or you can call them "baskets."

Let me break it down for you with an example. Imagine you have a friend who owns a fitness center, and let's call it "Fit & Strong Gym." This gym is pretty well-established, with a solid customer base and a thriving business structure. Now, what are the typical activities that Fit & Strong Gym might engage in?

Well, here are some of the business activities:

- First, they advertise to attract new customers. You might have seen their ads on social media or local billboards, encouraging people to join their fitness programs.

- Second, they hire fitness instructors to guide and help clients with their workouts. These instructors play a crucial role in ensuring everyone gets the right guidance and motivation.
- Third, sometimes the gym needs to buy new fitness equipment to replace the old ones. They want to provide their customers with the best tools and facilities for their workouts.

Next, let's talk about finances. Fit & Strong Gym might need some extra money for a short period. So, they could seek a short-term loan from a bank to cover those temporary expenses.

Alternatively, they could issue something called a "certificate of deposit" to raise funds. It's like borrowing money from people who want to invest in the gym and get a return on their investment later.

Now, let's think about expansion. Fit & Strong Gym wants to grow, so they decide to raise more capital for that. They might issue new shares to their friends or investors, which is called preferential allotment. By doing this, they can gather more money to expand their gym and reach more people.

On the other hand, sometimes they spot an exciting opportunity in a startup company working on innovative fitness regimes. So, they decide to invest some money in that startup to support their ideas and growth.

And, of course, just like we save money in a bank account, Fit & Strong Gym might also put some of their extra money in a fixed deposit for safekeeping.

Finally, they might come across a great building in the neighborhood that they want to use for opening another fitness center in the future. So, they decide to invest in buying that building.

Now, all these activities can be grouped into three baskets with a comprehensive list of transactions under each Activities:

i.   **Operating Activities:** It includes things like advertising, paying salaries to fitness instructors, and upgrading their services – basically, everything they do day-to-day to keep the gym running smoothly. Comprehensive list of transactions under operating Activities are as follows:

Cash flow from Operating Activities	
Receipts	Payments
• Cash Sales • Collection From Customers • Other income (exclude interest and dividend*) • Tax Refunds	• Payments to Suppliers • Payments for Expenses • (like Salaries & Wages, Staff Welfare, Electricity, Telephone, Travel, Professional Fees, Commission etc) • Other Payments (exclude interest) • Tax Payments

* Here is catch in Interest Income and Dividend Income, we have to be aware of the basics of each activity and objective, Let's break it down for better understanding:

- *For financial institutions (e.g., banks)*, cash flows arising from interest and dividends received should be classified as cash flows from operating activities. This is because such institutions primarily generate revenue from their core lending and investment activities, and interest and dividends are part of their regular operations.

- *For other entities (non-financial institutions)*, cash flows arising from interest and dividends received should be classified as cash flows from investing activities. This is because interest and dividends received are related to the company's investment activities and represent returns on investments made in other companies' securities.

Operating cash flow, measures the cash generated or used by a company's core business operations. It provides insights into how well a company's fundamental operations are generating cash flow before considering financing or investing activities. There are two primary methods to calculate operating cash flow which we will cover in next chapters:

- the Direct Method and
- the Indirect Method

ii. **Investing Activities**: This includes things like buying new fitness equipment and investing in that startup company. It's all about making investments for the future growth and success of the gym. Comprehensive list of transactions under Investing Activities are as follows:

Cash Flow From Investing Activities	
Receipts	Payments
• Sale of Assets • Sale of Investments • Receipts of loan Receivable • Interest Income Received • Dividend Received	• Payments for Assets Purchased • Purchase of long term investment • Fresh Loans given

iii. **Financing Activities**: Here, we have things like seeking a short-term loan, issuing certificates of deposit, and raising capital by issuing new shares. These activities are all about raising funds to support the gym's operations and expansion plans. Comprehensive list of transactions under Financing Activities are as follows:

Cash from Financing Activities	
Receipts	Payments
• Fresh infusion of capital • Borrowing Loans	• Loan repayments • Interest paid • Dividend paid

So, now that we have a clear understanding of these three baskets of activities. This statement will show us how money flows in and out of Fit & Strong Gym's business through these different activities. It's like a financial report card that helps us understand how financially healthy the gym is and how well they manage their cash.

Understanding these activities is essential because the cash flow statement is all about tracking the money in and out of a company. So, now that we've got the basics covered, let's dive into the fascinating world of the cash flow statement!

3.1 KEY REQUIREMENTS before Creating Cash Flow Statement

you know how sometimes, we struggle to get reliable and accurate data for our business, right? Well, the root cause of this issue is often simpler than we think. It's often because of improper accounting practices or delays in finishing the necessary work.

Let me explain it with a simple example. Imagine you're using some fancy accounting software to track your business's finances. You rely on this software to give you important information, like how much money you made in the last six months. Now, this software is really powerful and can spit out all those numbers for you with just one click! Sounds amazing, right?

But here's the catch. If the data you put into the software is wrong or incomplete, guess what you're gonna get? Yes, you guessed it! Garbage out. So, it's like the saying goes, 'garbage in, garbage out.' If you feed the system with flawed data, it's gonna give you flawed results.

So, the key here is to make sure that your books of account are complete and accurate. If you're not entering the right revenue or expense numbers, if you're missing some transactions, or if you're not reconciling accounts properly, the data you get from the software won't be worth much.

But don't worry, it's not all bad news. With automation and modern accounting software, it's become much easier to get valuable insights. Just make sure to keep your accounting in order, and then you can rely on the software to give you the right answers when you need them.

Remember, accurate data is the foundation of good decision-making. So, let's make sure to avoid that 'garbage in' situation, so we don't end up with 'garbage out' results!"

Here's the list of key requirements before creating cash flow statement:

1.   Get all your financial data ready, including a trial balance, which is a list of your accounts with their balances.

2.   Make sure all transactions are recorded correctly in your general ledger and sub-ledgers.

3.   Take care of closing entries, like moving income and expenses to retained earnings for the right period.

4.   If needed, make any adjusting entries for things like accruals, deferrals, and depreciation to match revenues and expenses properly.

5. Reconcile your bank statements to ensure everything is accurately recorded and there are no discrepancies.

6. Check the valuation of your inventory and make sure it matches the actual physical count.

7. Verify that your accounts receivable and payable balances are accurate and up-to-date.

8. Review your fixed asset records, including depreciation calculations.

9. If you have loans or debts, ensure their balances and interest payments are correctly recorded.

10. Make sure your revenue recognition follows the accounting standards.

11. Properly allocate expenses to the relevant periods.

12. Keep accounting principles and methods consistent with previous periods, unless there's a valid reason for change.

13. Be compliant with accounting standards and regulations for your industry or jurisdiction.

14. If you're using accounting software, ensure the formatting is accurate and follows standard presentation.

15. Set a deadline for completing the daily tasks, monthly reports and stick to it.

Remember, accuracy and completeness are crucial for financial statements, so make your checklist on your own or with your accountant, keeping above points in mind as per your business complexity and seeking professional advice from an financial expert is always a good idea if you're unsure about any aspect of the process.

UNLOCKING THE DIRECT METHOD 04

Analyzing Flow of Cash for Small Businesses

The beauty of the cash flow statement lies in its simplicity and clarity. Once completed, it provides a comprehensive overview of your business's financial dynamics, enabling you to make informed decisions and plan for the future effectively, much like learning to drive a car, it becomes easier with practice. When you're new to driving, there's a lot to remember—how to handle the steering wheel, pedals, gears, and navigate through traffic. It can feel overwhelming and challenging to stay in control.

Similarly, when you begin preparing a cash flow statement, you might feel unsure about where to start, what information to include, and how to categorize cash flows. It's like being in the driver's seat for the first time, unsure of the road ahead however, with patience and persistence, you start to get the hang of driving, and it becomes second nature. You become comfortable with the controls, anticipate turns, and react to different road conditions effortlessly.

Likewise, as you gain experience in preparing cash flow statements, you become more familiar with the cash movements in your business. You start to understand the ins and outs of cash flow, whether from operating activities, investing activities, or financing activities. It becomes a smooth process, much like driving a car once you've learned how to handle it.

In this chapter, I've introduced the first method of preparing a cash flow statement, which is called the Direct method. This method focuses on identifying the actual changes in cash receipts and payments that are reported in the cash flow statement. Both methods, Direct and Indirect, have their advantages, but the Direct method stands out for its simplicity and ease of understanding, making it accessible to business owners without extensive accounting knowledge or especially suitable for small businesses with fewer cash transactions.

Unlike the Indirect method, which involves adjusting net income for non-cash items and changes in working capital, the Direct method directly lists all cash receipts and disbursements. This straightforward approach provides a clear and concise picture of the cash inflows and outflows in a business.

First, Let's see the format of direct cash flow method:

4.1 Direct Method Format

M/s Zevroid Ventures		
Cash flow Statement for the year ended 31 March 20XX		
Particulars	Amount	Amount
Cash flow From Operating Activities		
Cash received:		
- Sale	XX	
-from customers	XX	XXX

M/s Zevroid Ventures		
Cash paid for:		
- Suppliers for Purchases	(XX)	
- Wages & Salary	(XX)	
- Operating and General administrative expenses	(XX)	
-Income Tax paid	(XX)	(XXX)
Net Cash flow from Operating Activities →	**A**	**XXX**
Cash flow from Investing Activities		
Cash received for:		
- Sale of Fixed Assets	XX	
- Sale of Investment	XX	
- Interest received	XX	
- Dividend received	XX	XXX
Cash paid for:		
- Purchase of Fixed Assets	(XX)	
- Purchase of Investments	(XX)	**(XXX)**
Net Cash Flow from Investing Activities →	**B**	**XXX**
Cash flow from Financing Activities		
Cash received for:	XX	
Issue of Equity Shares	XX	
Issue of Preference Share	XX	
Long term borrowings	XX	XXX
Cash paid for:		
- Interest paid	(XX)	
- Redemption of preference shares	(XX)	
- Repayment of Loans	(XX)	
Dividend paid	(XX)	**(XXX)**
Net Cash Flow from Financing Activities →	**C**	XXX
Total Cash flow from all Activities	**D=A+B+C**	XXX
Opening Cash/Bank Balances	**E**	XXX
Closing Cash/Bank Balance	**F=D+E**	XXX

Classification of transaction and preparing Cash flow from "direct method"

The process of preparing a cash flow statement from direct method is straightforward and doesn't require any specialized accounting knowledge. Anyone can do it with common sense. Here are the steps to create a cash flow statement for a month:

- **Step 1**: List down all the money you received and spent during the month on MS excel, whether it was through your bank account or cash. If you use accounting software like tally, you can easily export the details into MS Excel. Just remember to treat money received as positive figures and money spent as negative figures.
- **Step 2**: Once you have all the transactions in MS Excel, you need to classify them into three Activities which is Operating Activities, Investing Activities and Financing Activities. Simply classify whether each transaction is money received or spent it to the appropriate activities.
- **Step 3**: After classifying all the transactions, you'll need to add up the money in each Activities. Don't worry; Excel can help with that! You can use formulas like SUM or use Pivot Tables to quickly get the totals for each category.
- **Step 4**: Now, you have the net cash flow for each Activities. Just add up the net cash flow from Operating Activities, Investing Activities and Financing Activities to get the total cash flow for the month.

- **Step 5**: The last step is to check if the calculated total cash flow matches the change in your cash balance. If you had some cash at the beginning of the month, add the total cash flow to it. The result should be the same as your cash balance at the end of the month.

And there you have it! By following these simple steps, you can create a cash flow statement to understand how money flowed in and out of your accounts during the month. It's an essential tool for managing your finances and making informed decisions about your money.

Lets understand all above steps through detailed illustration:

S no.	Summary of cash transactions	Amount (Rs)
	Opening cash	50,000
1	Assets Purchased	(350,000)
2	Capital Introduced	100,000
3	Cash Sales	520,000
4	Collection from Customers	140,000
5	Dividend Income	1,500
6	FDR matured	120,000
7	Interest Income	8,000
8	Interest Paid	(60,000)
9	LIC premium paid	(20,000)
10	Loan Taken	500,000
11	Payment for Expenses	(200,000)
12	Payment to Suppliers	(600,000)
	Closing Cash	209,500

Above summary of cash transaction taken only for illustrative purpose.

Let's Classification of each transaction as define in above steps

S no.	Summary of cash transactions	Amount (Rs.)	Activities
1	Assets Purchased	(350,000)	Investing
2	Capital Introduced	100,000	Financing
3	Cash Sales	520,000	Operating
4	Collection from Customers	140,000	Operating
5	Dividend Income	1,500	Investing
6	FDR matured	120,000	Investing
7	Interest Income	8,000	Investing
8	Interest Paid	(60,000)	Financing
9	LIC premium paid	(20,000)	Financing
10	Loan Taken	500,000	Financing
11	Payment for Epenses	(200,000)	Operating
12	Payment to Suppliers	(600,000)	Operating

After classifying all the transactions, you'll need to Put each transaction as per the format provided above and add up the money in each Activities and add the total cash flow with opening balance of cash flow to get closing balance of Cash Balance.

Particulars	Add/(Less)	Total (Rs.)
Cash flow From Operating Activities	A	
Cash Sales	520,000	
Collection from Customers	140,000	
Payment to Suppliers	(600,000)	
Payment for Expenses	(200,000)	(140,000)
Cash flow from Investing Activities	B	
Assets Purchased	(350,000)	
Dividend Income	1,500	
Interest Income	8,000	
FDR matured	120,000	(220,500)
Cash flow from Financing Activities	C	
Interest Paid	(60,000)	
Capital Introduced	100,000	
Loan Taken	500,000	
LIC premium paid	(20,000)	520,000
Total Cash flow from all Activities	D=A+B+C	159,500
Opening Cash/Bank Balances	E	50,000
Closing Cash/Bank Balance	F=D+E	159,500

You realized! how easy, it is to prepare a cash flow using the direct method.

Certainly! Let's analyze the cash flow statement provided above:

1. **Cash Flow from Operating Activities:**
   - The company experienced a net cash outflow of Rs. 140,000 from operating activities. This means that during the specified period, the company spent more cash on its day-to-day operations (e.g., paying suppliers and expenses) than it received from cash sales and customer collections.

A negative operating cash flow can raise concerns about the company's ability to manage its working capital efficiently.

2. **Cash Flow from Investing Activities:**
   - The company experienced a net cash outflow of Rs. 220,500 from investing activities. This indicates that the company invested more cash in purchasing assets (e.g., equipment, machinery) than it received from dividends, interest income, and the maturity of the Fixed Deposit Receipt (FDR). This could be a sign of capital expenditures to support business growth, but it also means that the company is using cash to acquire long-term assets.

3. **Cash Flow from Financing Activities:**
   - The company experienced a net cash inflow of Rs. 520,000 from financing activities. This shows that the company raised cash by introducing capital, taking a loan, and received cash from financing activities. A positive cash flow from financing activities suggests that the company is obtaining funds to support its operations or expansion.

Overall Analysis: The cash flow statement shows that the company had a positive net cash flow of Rs. 159,500 during the specified period. This means that, overall, the company had more cash coming in than going out. The positive net cash flow from financing activities indicates that the company successfully raised funds to support its activities.

However, the negative cash flow from operating activities suggests that the company needs to closely manage its day-to-day cash flows and working capital to ensure smooth operations. It's important for the company to monitor and improve its operating cash flow to maintain financial stability and meet its short-term obligations.

The negative cash flow from investing activities indicates that the company is making significant investments in assets, which can be beneficial for long-term growth, but it also requires careful financial planning and management.

Regularly analyzing cash flow statements can help the company make informed decisions and take appropriate measures to ensure financial stability and growth.

INDIRECT METHOD DECODED

05

Making Sense of Cash Flow Adjustments

The direct method of preparing the cash flow statement was very easy to understand, wasn't it? Do you remember the example we discussed in the last chapter about learning to drive a car? Well, it actually applies here with indirect method because here, you practically implement the concept just like driving a car. Just like how you need to coordinate with accelerator, brake, and clutch while driving a car, preparing the cash flow statement using the indirect method of cash flow requires same coordination with the profit and loss account and balance sheet.

At the beginning, this method might not feel as easy, but once you grasp the concept, it becomes a quick and effective way to evaluate a company's cash flow alongside its financial performance.

The indirect method of cash flow is a technique used to adjust the net income by accounting, for changes resulting from non-cash transactions and working capital. It's commonly used by companies that undergo regular audits. Since it relies on information from Profit and loss statements and balance sheets, it can be quickly reviewed for accuracy.

It's often easier to prepare the cash flow statement using the indirect method with minimal effort because most organizations maintain their financial records on an accrual basis. This method establishes a direct link between the balance sheet and income statement, providing a more systematic view of the company's financial statements.

For larger companies with a high volume of daily transactions, using the indirect method can make the process of creating a cash flow statement more manageable. It allows for a comprehensive understanding of cash flows by adjusting net income to reflect the actual cash movements within the business.

Lets see the format of indirect method of cash flow to understand why we are making adjustments in indirect method and their connection with profit and loss account and balance sheet:

Particulars	Amount	Source	Reasons for required adjustment
Net Profit/ (Loss) as per Profit and Loss Account	XXX	P&L A/c	Net Profit/ (loss) should be after adjustment of taxes i.e PAT, if we have taken Profit before tax then we have adjust taxes from PBT
Add: Non-Cash Items like Depreciation Provisions for Doubtful Debtors/ Obsolete Inventory/ Warranty, etc. Bad Debts written off	XXX	P&L A/c	These are items in the profit and loss account that do not involve actual cash transactions, like depreciation (reduction in the value of assets over time) and provisions (estimations for potential future expenses). We add them back to the net profit because they don't affect cash flow.
Add: Interest Paid	XXX	P&L A/c	This is the amount of Cash paid as interest on loans or borrowings therefore interest expense is considered a cash outflow from financing activities.

Particulars	Amount	Source	Reasons for required adjustment
Add: Gain on sale of asset	XXX	P&L A/c	Gain on the sale of asset represents the profit made by the company on the sale of the asset. It is considered a non-operating activity and is added back to the net profit in the cash flow statement because it doesn't impact the company's core business operations.
Less: Loss on sale of assets	(XXX)	P&L A/c	Conversely, This loss represents the amount by which the sale proceeds are less than the asset's book value. Similar to the gain, the loss on the sale of a plant asset is also considered a non-operating activity and is added back to the net profit in the cash flow statement. It doesn't affect the company's core business operations
Less: Increase in Current Assets, i.e. Debtors/Stock/ Loans and Advances	(XXX)	Balance sheet	An increase in current assets means that more cash is tied up in assets like debtors, stock or loans and advances given to suppliers. We subtract this increase from the net profit because it represents cash that hasn't been received yet or is invested in inventory and advances. Such Increase should be reduced from profits to derive cash from operations
Add: Decrease in Current Assets, ie. Debtors/Stock/ Loans and Advances.	XXX	Balance sheet	Decrease in current assets, it means that cash invested in debtors, stock, or advances has been received during the period. We add this decrease to the net profit because it reflects cash received from these assets

Contd...

Particulars	Amount	Source	Reasons for required adjustment
Add: Increase in Current Liabilities, i.e. Creditors/ Expense Payable/Other Liabilities	XXX	Balance sheet	An increase in current liabilities shows that the company has accrued more expenses, like creditors or other liabilities, which are yet to be paid. We add this increase to the net profit because it represents cash that hasn't been paid out yet
Less: Decrease in Current Liabilities, i.e. Creditors/ Expense Payable/Other Liabilities	(XXX)	Balance sheet	Decrease in current liabilities indicates that old liabilities have been paid during the period. We subtract this decrease from the net profit because it shows cash paid out for those liabilities.
Cash from Operations	XXX		

If you look through the table and start correlating the 'Cash Balance' and 'Asset/Liability' you will observe that:

1. Whenever the asset of the company increases, the cash balance decreases. This means if the assets decreases, the cash balance increases.

2. Whenever the liabilities of the company increases, the cash balance also increases. This means if the liabilities decreases, the cash balance also decreases.

The above conclusion is the key concept while constructing a cash flow statement. Also, extending this further, you will realize that each company's activity is its operating activity, financing activity, or investing activity either produces cash (net increase in cash) or reduces (net decrease in cash)the cash for the company.

Both the direct method and indirect method of preparing the cash flow statement focus on the operating activities of the company. As a result, the investing and financing activities remain the same regardless of the method used. Except above adjustment, we have already covered other points of operating activities, investing and financing activities in previous chapter so there is nothing more to say on this.

Now Let me tell you a real-life story that will help you understand how the second method of preparing a cash flow statement works. So, there was this guy named Mr. Srinath, and he owned a product based IT company. One day, he was feeling really stressed because he couldn't figure out where all the money from his business had gone. It was like the funds just disappeared! To make matters worse, his company was running out of cash. It felt like they hit a roadblock, and they couldn't understand what went wrong. But you know what's interesting? When they checked their profit and loss account, it showed massive profits, and their sales were way higher than the previous year. So, on the surface, everything seemed great, and it looked like the business was booming. Their comparative profit and loss account looked as under:

PROFIT SYSTEMS PRIVATE LIMITED		
Statement of Profit and Loss for the year ended March 31, 2022		
(All amounts in Thousands, except otherwise specified)		
Particulars	**Year ending March 31, 2022**	**Period ending March 31, 2021**
Income		
Revenue from operations	67,628	58,674
Other Income	-	160
Total Income	67,628	**58,834**
Expenses		
Cost of materials purchased	55,566	50,447
Employee benefits expense	6,337	7,037
Changes in Inventories	(2,202)	(1,751)
Depreciation and amortization expense	438	322
Other expenses	3,073	2,455
Total Expense	63,212	58,511
Profit / (loss) before extraordinary item and tax	4,416	323
Extraordinary Item	-	-
Profit / (loss) before tax	4,416	323
Tax expense		
Current tax	1,148	116
Deferred Tax	(46)	32
Total tax expense	1,102	148
Profit / (loss) after tax	3,314	239
Earning / (loss) per equity share: [nominal value of share Rs. 10]		
Basic (Rs)	18.41	1.40
Diluted (Rs)	18.41	1.40

To figure out what was happening, we delved into the situation. We examined the profit and loss account, which showed a substantial increase in net profits compared to the previous year. So, why was the business short of funds? When I asked him about it, he was baffled and frustrated. He believed that the accounts department should have been more proactive, and if they had been, the company wouldn't be facing this cash crunch. It was clear that something wasn't adding up between the impressive profits on paper and the lack of funds in the company's accounts. We needed to investigate further to uncover the underlying reasons. Now, We decided to scrutinize the balance sheet next which is as follows:

PROFIT SYSTEMS PRIVATE LIMITED		
Balance Sheet as at 31st March 2022		
(All amounts in Thousands, except otherwise specified)		
Particulars	As at March 31, 2022	As at March 31, 2021
A. EQUITY AND LIABILITIES		
(1) Shareholder's Funds		
(a) Share Capital	1,800	1,710
(b) Reserves and Surplus	3,622	308
	5,422	2,018
(2) Non Current Liabilities		
(a) Secured Loan from Bank	6,981	804
(b) Unsecured Loan from Directors	1,333	3,320
	8,314	4,124
(3) Current Liabilities		
(a) Trade payables	13,827	11,380
(b) Other current liabilities	5,085	4,646
	18,912	16,027
Total	32,648	22,168

Contd...

PROFIT SYSTEMS PRIVATE LIMITED		
B. ASSETS		
(1) Non-current assets		
(a) Property, Plants & Equipments	766	712
(b)Non Current Investments	688	300
(c) Deferred Tax Assets	178	132
	1,633	**1,145**
(2) Current assets		
(a) Trade receivables	10,440	6,575
(b) Cash and bank balances	62	381
(c) Inventories	15,855	12,653
(d) Other Current Assets	4,659	1,415
	31,016	**21,023**
Total	**32,648**	**22,168**

Looking at the balance sheet, it was evident that the amount owed by debtors had increased compared to the previous year, and the stock and other current Assets held by the company was also much higher. But this was understandable because the company's sales had significantly gone up, leading to higher receivables and stock levels.

Moreover, the company had used its substantial profits to repay loans, which was a smart financial decision. By reducing interest costs, the company would have even more profits available for the owners in the future.

Interestingly, the company now had higher cash credit limits from the bank, which allowed them to take advantage of early payment to suppliers and receive substantial cash discounts on purchases. So, while it appeared that the amount owed to creditors had increased, in reality, it was just a strategic move to maximize cash savings.

Upon analyzing the balance sheet and profit and loss account, we didn't find anything alarming or adverse. However, we realized that to understand the actual movement of funds, we needed to prepare a cash flow statement. Because we have ready available profit and loss A/c and balance sheet So, we proceeded with Indirect method to create the cash flow statement and gain more insights into the company's cash flow situation.

PROFIT SYSTEMS PRIVATE LIMITED	
Cash Flow Statement for the year ended March 31, 2022	
(All amounts in Thousands, except otherwise specified)	
Particulars	**For the year ended on March 31, 2022**
Cash flows from operating activities	
Profit/ (Loss) before tax from continuing operations	4,416
Adjustments for:	
Depreciation and amortization expenses	438
Interest charged	710
Operating Profit/(Loss) before working capital changes	**5,564**
Changes in working capital:	
(Increase)/Decrease in trade receivables	(3,865)
(Increase)/Decrease in Inventories	(3,202)
(Increase)/Decrease in other current assets	(3,244)
Increase/(Decrease) in Trade payables	2,447
Increase/(Decrease) in Other liabilities	439
Net cash generated from/ (used in) operations	**(1,861)**
Income tax payment (including TDS)	(1,148)
Net cash flow from/(used in) operating activities (A)	**(3,009)**
Cash flows from investment activities	
Purchase of fixed assets	(492)
Purchase of Investments	(388)
Net cash generated from/ (used in) investing activities (B)	**(880)**

Contd…

PROFIT SYSTEMS PRIVATE LIMITED	
Cash flows from financing activities	
Proceeds from issuance of equity share capital	90
Proceeds from Secured Loan from Banks	6,177
Repayment of Unsecured Loan from Directors	(1,987)
Interest paid on loan	(710)
Net cash generated from/ (used in) financing activities (C)	**3,571**
Net increase/(decrease) in cash/cash equivalents (A+B+C)	**(318)**
Cash and Cash Equivalents at beginning of the year	381
Cash and Cash Equivalents at end of the year	62

You know what we found? Even though the company showed impressive profits on paper, they were facing a cash crunch. It was like all the money they earned was stuck somewhere and not flowing in as cash. So, even with those big profits, they could generate negative cash flow from their operations The main problem was that a lot of their money was tied up in three things: debtors (people who owed them money),stock and other current Assets. You see, to boost sales, they extended credit to customers, allowing them more time to pay. But this meant that the money they earned from sales was not coming in right away.

On the other hand, to take advantage of cash discounts offered by suppliers, they had stocked up on raw materials and packaging materials. So, their factory was filled with piles of inventory. While this was a good strategy to save money on purchases, it tied up a lot of their cash in the form of stock.

Hold on a second! Something caught our attention. Despite the increased overdraft (OD) limit from the bank, the cash flows from financing activities were surprisingly low. As we dug deeper into the cash flow statement, we noticed that loans worth INR 1,987 thousands were repaid during the year. But here's the interesting part: these were unsecured loans taken from the Directors (business owner).

Naturally, I asked Mr. Srinath why they repaid those loans. And he explained that they were excited by the big profits and also as additional working capital was financed through bank, they felt they could withdraw their money without affecting the company's cash flows. To some extent, Mr. Srinath's thinking was reasonable. However, the problem arose when they overlooked the fact that their cash from operations needed to be positive alongside the impressive profit numbers. Profit on paper doesn't necessarily mean there's enough cash to handle their day-to-day expenses.

It's like having a high-paying job but spending all the money on fancy things without setting aside some savings. You might seem wealthy, but if you're not managing your cash flow properly, you could still end up in financial trouble.

So, even with the bank's help, they didn't pay enough attention to their cash flow from operations, which is a crucial aspect of financial health. And that's what led to the cash crunch and the confusion they faced despite those eye-catching profits.

So, to fix the situation, they took action. They improved their collections process and found ways to manage inventory better. And you know what? It worked! Their cash flow got much better, and they were no longer facing that dreadful cash crunch.

In the end, this real-life story taught us the importance of preparing a cash flow statement using the indirect method. It helped Mr. Srinath understand the real cash position of his business and enabled him to make smart decisions to improve cash flow and keep his product based IT company financially healthy.

ANALYSIS AND IMPROVE 06

Just because a business shows a high profit or positive cash flow doesn't always mean it's running smoothly without any issues. There could be underlying flaws that need attention. Similarly, having negative cash flow doesn't necessarily imply that the business is in trouble. Let's delve deeper into this concept in a conversational manner:

We have to look **Beyond the Numbers - Understanding the Real Story Behind Profits** and Cash Flow. We often assume that a business with high profits or positive cash flow is doing fantastic, while one with negative cash flow is doomed. Well, it's not that simple! Let's unravel the truth together!'

You must heard about this proverb **"Not All That Glitters is Gold"**. The Hidden Side of Positive Cash Flow: Positive cash flow sounds like a dream, right? It means you have more money coming in than going out. But wait a minute! What if you're borrowing money to maintain that cash flow? Taking out loans or using credit might boost your cash flow for now, but it also means you have debt to pay off later. So, while it looks good on the surface, you've got to watch out for the hidden implications.

When you see negative cash flow, it's a sign that something needs fixing. It's like a warning light on your car's dashboard - you need to pay attention! Maybe your expenses are skyrocketing, or your customers are slow in paying you. You've got to identify those leaks and patch them up!

but, **Negative Cash Flow Isn't Always a Red Flag,** It's like the black sheep of the financial family. Yes, it can raise concerns, but it's not the end of the world. Negative cash flow might occur for various reasons. For instance, you might be investing in your business to upgrade equipment, expand to new locations, or launch exciting products. These investments are crucial for growth, but they can temporarily impact cash flow.

Negative cash flow resulting from **investments in the business can be a positive thing**. You are spending money now to make more money later. It's like planting a seed to grow a bigger tree that bears more fruit. Smart businesses often take such calculated risks to grow and expand.

Sometimes, **negative cash flow can be temporary**. For instance, during seasonal sales fluctuations, your bakery might have a few slow months, causing negative cash flow. But when the busy season hits, sales soar, and the cash flow **turns positive again**.

Running a business is like walking on a tightrope. You've got to **balance the art of making profits with managing cash flow**. Sometimes, that might mean making short-term sacrifices for long-term gains. So, don't panic if you encounter negative cash flow. Take a step back, assess the situation, and make informed decisions.

Profits and positive cash flow are essential, but they don't paint the full picture. There could be hidden expenses eating into those profits or could be we are purchasing big liability to come out from another small liability. Temporary investments causing negative cash flow. What truly matters is **understanding the reasons behind the numbers and taking proactive steps to improve** your business operations.

We will understand this chapter through 2 illustrations by which We need to get down to the nitty-gritty and consider every aspect of your business that affects cash flow.

6.1 Illustration 1

Let's create first illustration where net cash generate from cash flow and closing cash balance are very high as compare to another company where net cash generate from cash flow is negative and closing cash balance are very low against opening cash balance. we try to develop that understanding which help us in analyzing cash flow, their impact and points where improvement required. Their comparative Cash flow looked as under:

Particulars	ABC Ltd.	XYZ Ltd.
Operating activities		
Net Income	(225,000)	225,000
Adjustments to reconcile net income		
depreciation and amortization	15,000	50,000
Gain on sale of investment	(227,800)	
Increase in accounts receivable	(57,500)	5,550
decrease in inventory	(36,250)	(221,250)
Increase in accounts payable	1,100	(15,150)
decrease in income taxes payable	(9,500)	(13,900)
Net cash provided by operating activities	**(539,950)**	**30,250**
Investing Activities		
Purchase of new plant		(500,000)
Sale of Investment	400,000	
Net cash used for investing activities	**400,000**	**(500,000)**
Financing Activities		
Issue of shares		400,000
Proceeds from long term borrowings	250,000	
Net cash provided by financing activities	**250,000**	**400,000**
Net Increase (Decrease) in cash flow	**110,050**	**(69,750)**
Beginning of year	**10,000**	**100,000**
End of year	**120,050**	**30,250**

let's analyze the cash flow statements of ABC Ltd. and XYZ Ltd. and suggest improvements for both companies.

6.1.1 Analysis of ABC Ltd.'s Cash Flow

- ABC Ltd. is facing negative net cash flow from operating activities, indicating that they are not generating enough cash from their core business operations to cover their expenses.
- The company's profit as per the income statement is coming from gains on the sale of investments,

not from their primary business activities. This shows a reliance on non-core income sources.

- ABC Ltd. had to take loans to maintain their cash balance, which could lead to increased financial obligations in the future.

6.1.2 Suggestions for Improvement - ABC Ltd.

1. Focus on Core Business: ABC Ltd. should prioritize improving its core business operations to generate positive cash flow from day-to-day activities. This can be achieved through better sales strategies, cost optimization, and efficient inventory management.

2. Reduce Reliance on Investment Gains: While occasional gains on investments are okay, the primary focus should be on profitability from core business activities. ABC Ltd. should aim to make profits from its products or services, not just from asset sales.

3. Better Cash Flow Management: The company should work on maintaining a healthy cash flow without relying on loans. Improved cash flow management will help reduce debt and increase financial stability.

6.1.3 Analysis of XYZ Ltd.'s Cash Flow

- XYZ Ltd. has positive net cash flow from operating activities, indicating that they are successfully generating cash from their core business operations to cover expenses.
- The company is raising capital to invest in machinery and inventory which demonstrates a stable and sustainable income source in future.
- However, there is a decrease in cash flow from the previous year, which needs attention to maintain financial strength.

6.1.4   Suggestions for Improvement - XYZ Ltd.

1. Maintain Strong Operating Cash Flow: XYZ Ltd. should continue focusing on its core business operations to sustain a strong cash flow. Regularly analyzing the performance of operating activities and making necessary adjustments will ensure consistent positive cash flow.

2. Diversification and Growth: company shows positive sign by expanding business and generating negative cash flow doesn't necessarily indicate a red flag for the company.

3. Cash Flow Forecasting: Implementing cash flow forecasting will enable XYZ Ltd. to anticipate potential fluctuations in cash flow and plan for contingencies. This proactive approach will help in effectively managing financial resources.

In conclusion, ABC Ltd. needs to focus on improving its core business operations, reducing reliance on investment gains, and better cash flow management. On the other hand, XYZ Ltd. should maintain its strong operating cash flow, explore opportunities for growth, and implement cash flow forecasting to ensure financial stability and sustainable growth.

6.2   Illustration 2

Now create one illustration where profit, Opening cash flow, net cash generate from cash flow and closing cash balance, all are same and then we will compare two cash flow statement of different company and try to develop that understanding which help us in analyzing cash flow, their impact and points where improvement required. Their comparative Cash flow looked as under:

Particulars	ABC Ltd.	XYZ Ltd.
Operating activities		
Net Income	125,000	125,000
Adjustments to reconcile net income		
depreciation and amortization	15,000	200,000
Gain on sale of equipment	(227,800)	-
Increase in accounts receivable	(107,500)	55,550
decrease in inventory	36,250	(121,250)
Increase in accounts payable	1,100	(15,150)
decrease in income taxes payable	(9,500)	(13,900)
Net cash provided by operating activities	**(167,450)**	**230,250**
Investing Activities		
Sale of equipment	287,350	(20,600)
Net cash used for investing activities	**287,350**	**(20,600)**
Financing Activities		
Proceeds from long term borrowings	40,000	(49,750)
Net cash provided by financing activities	**40,000**	**(49,750)**
Net Increase (Decrease) in cash flow	**159,900**	**159,900**
Beginning of year	**50,000**	**50,000**
End of year	**209,900**	**209,900**

So, first up, ABC Ltd. When we checked their cash flow statement, we noticed that the net cash generated from their operations was in the negative territory. Now, that's not a good sign! It means they're not making enough money from their core business activities to cover their expenses. And guess what? Their profit, as shown in the income statement, actually came from the gain they made on selling investments. So, it's not from their main business operations. On top of that, we saw that ABC Ltd. had to take out loans just to keep their cash balance at the same level. So, it looks like they're sort of juggling things around to keep things afloat.

Now, let's shift our focus to XYZ Ltd. When we glanced at their cash flow statement, it was like a breath of fresh air! Their cash flow from operations was strong at 230,250. That's a good sign! It means they're making enough money from their day-to-day business activities to cover their expenses even they are paying off their loans which generate more cash for stake holders. They're not relying on any one-time gains or selling off equipment to generate cash. They seem to have a steady flow of income from their main business operations, which is a great position to be in.

Absolutely! ABC Ltd. should focus on its core operations and work towards generating cash flow from them. To do that, they need to invest in marketing to attract more customers and boost sales. By spending money wisely on effective marketing strategies. They should also pay attention to is improving debtor realization. This means they should work on getting their customers to pay their dues on time. Sometimes, slow-paying customers can cause cash flow problems, so ABC Ltd. needs to implement better credit management practices and follow up with customers to ensure timely payments. By concentrating on these areas, ABC Ltd. can enhance its cash flow and strengthen its financial position. Remember, a well-run and successful business focuses on its core operations and ensures that the cash flow generated from those operations is steady and sustainable. So, let's see ABC Ltd. invest in its future by taking care of its operations and optimizing cash flow!

As Conclusion, looking at the first illustration, we realized that ABC Ltd. initially appeared to have everything going positively. However, upon closer analysis, it turned out that they were heading in a negative direction and needed a lot of improvements to be made. On the contrary, XYZ Ltd., which seemed negative at first, had a valid explanation for its situation - it was due to their business expansion, not any inherent weaknesses.

Now, let's take a look at another illustration where, on the surface, both companies appeared to be the same, but the real picture inside was entirely different. ABC Ltd. seemed weak internally, but it had strategically placed window dressing to compete with XYZ Ltd.

This illustration highlights the importance of conducting a thorough analysis of a company's financial statements and operations beyond what meets the eye. Relying solely on surface-level observations can be misleading, as the real story lies within the details. So, it's essential for business owners to adopt a perspective from the standpoint of investors and stakeholders. By doing so, they can gain valuable insights into how external parties perceive their business. This fresh perspective can reveal strengths and weaknesses that might not be immediately apparent to those closely involved in the day-to-day operations.

CASH FLOW PROJECTION AND TIMELY REVIEW

07

You know, when it comes to financial projections, many business owners just see it as some sort of paperwork exercise. They think it's just something the bank needs to renew their credit limits, so they pass it off to their accountants or a chartered accountant firm, and that's that.

The thing is, most of these business owners always ignore to make these projected financial statements for anything beyond satisfying the bank. They don't use it to monitor their own business's growth and profitability. Sure, they might have some sales and profit targets in mind, but preparing a detailed projected balance sheet and profit and loss account? Nah, that's too much effort for them.

And reviewing their actual performance against those projections? Forget about it! They just don't want to put in that kind of work. It's a lack of willingness, you see.

But here's the thing, once you actually do these projections and then take a look at how your business is really doing, you can start to see where you're falling short. It's like shining a light on your weaknesses.

Maybe you're not hitting the sales figures you thought you would, or your profits are not where they should be. It gives you a reality check and shows you where your business is lacking.

And that's valuable information! It gives you a chance to course-correct, to make changes and improvements, and get your business back on track. It's like having a roadmap for success and being able to navigate your way to it.

So, yeah, I get it. Making financial projections might not be the most exciting task, and it does take some effort. But trust me, it's worth it. It's a tool that can help you understand your business better, make smarter decisions, and ultimately, achieve those goals you set for yourself.

So, if you're a business owner, don't just brush off financial projections as some boring requirement. Embrace it, use it, and let it guide you towards success. You'll thank yourself later when you see your business thriving and reaching new heights.

Creating a cash flow projection for your business involves several steps. Here's a step-by-step guide to help you through the process:

1. **Gather Financial Data:** Collect all relevant financial data from your business records, including historical cash flow statements, income statements, and balance sheets. If you're just starting your business and don't have historical data, focus on estimating future cash flows based on your business plan and market research. Here are two examples of the financial data you might gather:

Example 1: Small Coffee Shop

Assume you run a Coffee shop. You've been in business for two years and have kept detailed financial records. Here's the data you might gather:

- Historical Cash Flow Statements: Collect cash flow statements for the past two years, which show the actual cash inflows and outflows for each month. This data will help you identify any seasonal trends or patterns in your cash flow.
- Income Statements (Profit and Loss Statements): Obtain income statements for the past two years, which show your revenues, expenses, and net income. This data will be useful to cross-reference with cash flow statements and ensure consistency.
- Balance Sheets: Collect balance sheets for the past two years, which provide a snapshot of your business's assets, liabilities, and equity at a specific point in time. While not directly related to cash flow, balance sheets can help you assess your business's financial position.

Example 2: Tech Startup

Imagine you're the founder of a tech startup that just launched six months ago. As a startup, you don't have historical financial data. In this case, you might consider the following data sources:

- Business Plan Projections: Refer to the financial projections you made in your business plan before launching the startup. Your business plan should have estimated future revenues, expenses, and potential funding sources, which can serve as the basis for your initial cash flow projections.

- Market Research: Conduct market research to gather data on industry benchmarks, competitor performance, and potential sales opportunities. This research can help you make more informed assumptions about your cash inflows and outflows.
- Budget and Expense Tracking: Since you have been operating for six months, you can track your actual expenses and cash inflows during this period. Use this data as a starting point to project future cash flows. Keep in mind that the data is limited, but it can still be valuable for initial projections.

Remember, the accuracy of your cash flow projections depends on the quality and completeness of the data you gather. If you have historical financial data, use it to identify trends and patterns. If you're a startup, make informed assumptions based on your business plan, market research, and any actual data you've collected during the initial period of operation.

2. **Identify and Estimate Cash Inflows:** List all potential sources of cash inflows for your business. These may include sales revenue, accounts receivable collections, interest income, loans, or any other sources of money coming into your business and estimating cash inflows involves making assumptions based on historical data (if available), market research, and your business's growth prospects. Here are two examples of cash inflow sources for different types of businesses:

Example 1: Coffee Shop

Imagine you own a small coffee shop in a busy neighborhood. Let's identify and estimate cash inflows for your coffee shop:

- **Cash Inflow Source: Daily Sales**
  - Identify the primary source of cash inflow: revenue from daily sales of coffee, pastries, and other menu items.
  - Estimate daily sales based on historical data or industry benchmarks.
  - Assume that cash payments and credit/debit card transactions contribute to cash inflows.

- **Cash Inflow Source: Catering Services**
  - If your coffee shop provides catering services, estimate the number of catering orders you expect to receive each month.
  - Calculate the average revenue per catering order to determine the monthly cash inflow from catering services.

- **Cash Inflow Source: Gift Cards and Loyalty Programs**
  - If your coffee shop offers gift cards or loyalty programs, estimate the monthly revenue generated from gift card sales and redeemed loyalty points.

- **Cash Inflow Source: Online Orders**
  - If your coffee shop accepts online orders for pick-up or delivery, estimate the monthly revenue from online sales.

3. **Identify and Estimate Cash Outflows:** List all regular and one-time cash outflows your business is likely to incur. These may include expenses like rent, utilities, salaries, inventory purchases, loan repayments, and other operational costs. Similar to cash inflows, estimate the amount of cash you expect to pay for each expense on a monthly basis. Again, be realistic and consider any seasonal or one-time expenses. Let's continue with the coffee shop example:

Example: Coffee Shop

- **Cash Outflow: Cost of Goods Sold (COGS)**
  - Estimate the cost of coffee beans, milk, pastries, and other ingredients required to prepare your menu items.
  - Consider historical data and supplier pricing to calculate the average monthly COGS.

- **Cash Outflow: Labor Expenses**
  - Include wages for baristas, kitchen staff, and other employees involved in the coffee shop's daily operations.
  - Factor in any additional labor costs, such as overtime or temporary staff during peak hours or special events.

- **Cash Outflow: Rent and Utilities**
  - Estimate the monthly rent and utility expenses for your coffee shop space.
  - Consider electricity, water, internet, and other utility costs.

- **Cash Outflow: Equipment and Maintenance**
  - Include any one-time or recurring expenses related to coffee machines, grinders, kitchen equipment, and furniture.

- o Account for regular maintenance costs to ensure the equipment's proper functioning.

- **Cash Outflow: Inventory Purchases**
  - o Estimate the amount required to replenish inventory, including coffee beans, milk, syrups, pastries, and other consumables.
  - o Consider the frequency of inventory purchases based on sales volume and expiration dates.

- **Cash Outflow: Marketing and Advertising**
  - o Allocate a budget for marketing and advertising efforts to attract new customers and promote your coffee shop.
  - o Consider social media advertising, local promotions, and other marketing strategies.

- **Cash Outflow: Staff Benefits and Taxes**
  - o Account for any additional expenses related to staff benefits, such as health insurance or paid leave.
  - o Include payroll taxes and other employment-related costs.

- **Cash Outflow: Contingency Fund**
  - o Set aside a portion of your projected revenue as a contingency fund to cover unexpected expenses or emergencies.

- **Cash Outflow: Loan Repayments (if applicable)**
  - o If your coffee shop has taken out a loan, include the monthly loan repayments in your cash outflows.

4. **Calculate Net Cash Flow:** Once you have your projected cash and expenses, you can calculate the company's projected cash flow using the following equation:

    Projected cash flow = total projected cash - total projected expenses

    The total project cash is incoming, and the total project expenses are outgoing. The projected cash flow figure could be positive or negative, depending on which of the incoming or outgoing cash amounts are higher.

5. **Add the projected cash flow figure to the current cash amount:** If the company's cash flow is positive, add this number to your opening balance to calculate the next month's opening figure. If it's negative, subtract the cash flow amount. This figure can help you identify if the company earns enough money during future pay periods to cover its expenses and make a profit. If you're calculating monthly, this figure can be the opening cash amount for the following month.

6. **Other Points keep in mind while creating cash flow projections: you can also consider some other factors to make cash flow more realistic as follows:**

    - **Consider Non-Cash Items:** Remember that some items in your income statement might not affect your cash flow directly (e.g., depreciation). Take these into account when projecting cash flows.
    - **Include Cash Reserves:** If you plan to maintain a cash reserve for emergencies or working capital needs, factor this into your projections. Ensure your

cash reserve is sufficient to cover any unexpected downturns.

- **Adjust for Seasonality:** If your business experiences seasonal fluctuations in cash flow, adjust your projections accordingly. Take into account how different months might have higher or lower cash inflows and outflows.
- **Scenario Planning:** Perform scenario analysis to evaluate the impact of different situations on your cash flow. For example, model how your cash flow would be affected if sales increase by a certain percentage or if there's a delay in customer payments.

7.1   Sample Cash flow projection statement

Here's a sample of a cash flow projection scenario and statement:

Neha wants to create a cash flow projection for the second half of the year to ensure she has enough cash to cover her expenses and still earn a profit. At the end of June, her business has 10,000 in cash. She creates a projected cash flow statement with all her projected income and expenses for July through December:

	July	August	September	October	November	December
Starting Cash balance (A)	10,000	14,400	14,100	15,200	14,400	14,400
Incoming cash						
Sales	5,000	2,000	3,000	1,000	1,000	4,000
Credit payments	1,000	-	500	-	500	500
Total incoming cash Flow (B)	6,000	2,000	3,500	1,000	1,500	4,500
Outgoing cash						
Rent	1,000	1,000	1,000	1,000	1,000	1,000
Utilities	400	500	400	400	400	800
Marketing	200	800	1,000	400	100	400
Total Outgoing Cash flow (C)	1,600	2,300	2,400	1,800	1,500	2,200
Ending balance (A+B-C)	14,400	14,100	15,200	14,400	14,400	16,700

Neha's projected cash flow for the second half of the year is ₹6,700. Using these projections, she might calculate some additional investments she can make to increase her cash flow.

I suggest that you make the projections as detailed as possible. every line item have valid base of assumptions. let me explain why the beauty of a projected cash flow statement lies in the details and why having valid assumptions for each line item is crucial.

To create an accurate projection, you need to get down to the nitty-gritty and consider every aspect of your business that affects cash flow. Think about your sales revenue, expenses, and all the factors that can impact your financial health So, we can say that we has to dig down deep to find the real reasons by breaking down expenses to the lowest levels possible.

Each line item in your cash flow projection must have a valid base of assumptions. You can't just guess or rely on wishful thinking. Instead, look at historical data, market trends, and your business's performance to make realistic estimates.

Let's take a coffee shop as an example. You'll need to think about how much money you expect to make from coffee and pastry sales each month. Consider the costs of ingredients, labor, rent, utilities, equipment, and everything else involved in running the shop. But don't stop there! Assumptions should be backed by some data base, some example of assumptions as follows:

Examples	Assumptions or Details
Sales and Revenue Growth	10% annual growth in sales
Payment Terms	Average 30 days for accounts receivable
Cost of Goods Sold (COGS)	10,000 per month for raw materials and labor
Operating Expenses	5,000 per month for rent, utilities, and salaries
Seasonality	20% higher sales in Q4 due to holiday season
Inventory Management	Maintain inventory at two months' worth of sales
Capital Expenditures	50,000 for new machinery in Q3
Debt Payments	1,000 monthly loan payment with 5% interest
Tax Payments	Quarterly income tax payment of 6,000
Economic Conditions	Assume a stable economy with 2% inflation rate
Contingency Planning	Include a 5% buffer for unexpected expenses
Accounts Payable	Average 45 days to pay bills and accounts payable

If you miss any of these details or make assumptions without a strong foundation, your cash flow projection might not reflect the reality. You could end up with unexpected cash shortages or miss out on opportunities for growth.

By paying attention to every line item, you can spot potential cash flow gaps and plan for them in advance. Maybe you'll realize that you need to build up a cash reserve or adjust your expenses during slower months. Having valid assumptions also helps you create contingency plans for unforeseen circumstances.

So, don't rush through your projected cash flow statement. Take the time to dig into the details, analyze your data, and make informed estimates. The more comprehensive and accurate your projection is, the better equipped you'll be to steer your business towards success and financial stability. Remember, the beauty of a well-crafted cash flow projection lies in its ability to guide you through the ups and downs of business with confidence and clarity.

7.1.1   Review and Revise

When you create a projected cash flow statement for your business, you're essentially making educated guesses about your future financial situation. But as we all know, the future is unpredictable! That's why "Review and Revise" comes in.

Once you have your projected cash flow in hand, the journey doesn't stop there. You need to regularly review how your business is actually performing and compare it to your projections. This review process helps you see if your assumptions were accurate and identify any deviations from your plans.

Think of it as a reality check for your business. Are you bringing in the expected cash? Are your expenses in line with what you projected? By reviewing your cash flow regularly, you'll catch any discrepancies early on and have a chance to correct them.

The next step is to revise your cash flow projections based on the insights you gained during the review. Maybe you overestimated your sales for a particular month or didn't account for a new expense. No worries! It happens to the best of us.

By revising your projections, you're making them more accurate and realistic. You'll be able to make better-informed decisions about your business's financial future. It's like adjusting your sails when the winds change direction to keep your business on course.

"Correcting yourself by Review and Revise of projected cash flow" is a valuable practice for any business owner. It allows you to be proactive and stay ahead of potential financial challenges. Plus, it gives you peace of mind knowing that you're aware of your business's financial health and taking steps to steer it in the right direction. Let's illustrate with an example of a small retail store.

7.1.2   Example: Small Retail Store

Month	Projected Cash Inflows	Actual Cash Inflows	Projected Cash Outflows	Actual Cash Outflows	Net Cash Flow (Projected)	Net Cash Flow (Actual)
February	Sales Revenue: 16,500	Sales Revenue: 16,800	Cost of Goods Sold (COGS): 6,800	Cost of Goods Sold (COGS): 6,600	9,700	10,200
	Other Income: 1,200	Other Income: 1,000	Labor Expenses: 3,200	Labor Expenses: 3,000		
			Rent and Utilities: 1,500	Rent and Utilities: 1,500		
			Marketing Expenses: 900	Marketing Expenses: 950		
			Miscellaneous Expenses: 700	Miscellaneous Expenses: 650		
March	Sales Revenue: 17,000	-	Cost of Goods Sold (COGS): 7,000	-	10,000	-
	Other Income: 1,000	-	Labor Expenses: 3,200	-		-
			Rent and Utilities: 1,500	-		-
			Marketing Expenses: 950	-		-
			Miscellaneous Expenses: 700	-		-

7.1.3   February Review and Revision

At the end of February, you review your cash flow statement. Your sales revenue for February exceeded your revised projection due to a successful Valentine's Day promotion, resulting in higher net cash flow. However, your actual marketing expenses were slightly higher than projected due to an unexpected increase in advertising costs.

7.1.4   March Projection

As of February, the actual cash inflows and outflows for March are yet to be determined. The projected net cash flow for March remains at 10,000, but it's subject to change based on the actual financial performance.

Remember, there's no shame in making adjustments to your cash flow projections. In fact, it's a sign of good financial management. The business world is dynamic, and staying flexible is essential for success.

In conclusion, "Correcting yourself by Review and Revise of projected cash flow" is all about staying in tune with your business's financial reality. Embrace this practice, and you'll have a clearer picture of your financial journey, making it easier to navigate the ups and downs of running a successful business. So, review, revise, and keep your business sailing towards a prosperous future!

PRICE TO CASH FLOW

08

Business owners! If you've made it this far in the book, you must have gained some valuable insights into cash flow and its significance in running a successful business. You now understand how important this tool can be, in maintaining a strong business foundation. So far, we've understand how to use cash flow to manage our own business effectively.

This chapter as a valuable resource to expand our knowledge of the business world. Understanding, how to assess and value other businesses will empower us to make informed decisions and enhance our own business strategies. Only then can we truly appreciate the worth of our own business in the eyes of others. It also helps us become better negotiators when discussing deals or collaborations with other companies because every business is unique, and so are its valuation metrics.

Now, I want to share some insights that can help you understand how investors look at your company's valuation and why they consider these two important financial ratios.

8.1 Price-to-Earnings Ratio

Let's discuss the P/E ratio or the price-to-earnings ratio. I'm sure many of you are familiar with this term because if you've ever invested in the stock market, you must have heard experts talking about it. They might say something like, "The P/E ratio of a particular stock has come down significantly, indicating that the price is undervalued, making it a good time to invest. On the other hand, the P/E ratio of another stock has increased significantly, suggesting that the price has become overvalued."

The price-to-earnings ratio (P/E ratio) is a valuation metric used to assess the relative value of a company's stock by comparing its market price per share to its earnings per share (EPS) We have already understand in detail about EPS in chapter 2. It is one of the most commonly used financial ratios for evaluating a company's attractiveness as an investment.

The formula for calculating the price-to-earnings ratio is:

P/E ratio = Market Price per Share / Earnings per Share (EPS)

Where:

- Market Price per Share is the current stock price of the company.
- Earnings per Share (EPS) is the company's total earnings divided by the number of outstanding shares.

The P/E ratio indicates how much investors are willing to pay for each rupee of earnings generated by the company. A higher P/E ratio suggests that investors have higher expectations for future earnings growth, and they are willing to pay a premium for the stock. Conversely, a lower P/E ratio may indicate that investors have lower growth expectations or concerns about the company's prospects.

It's essential to use the P/E ratio in conjunction with other financial metrics and qualitative analysis to make well-informed investment decisions. Also, be aware that P/E ratios can fluctuate over time based on changes in the company's earnings and stock price. Earnings can also sometimes be influenced by accounting practices, which can sometimes make them a bit less reliable. For example, a company might use certain accounting tricks or one-time events to inflate its earnings temporarily. That's why savvy investors don't rely solely on the P/E ratio; they take a more comprehensive approach.

8.2 Price-to-Cash Flow Ratio

Now, let's move on to the P/CF ratio or the price-to-cash flow ratio. This ratio is a bit different from the P/E ratio because it focuses on our operating cash flow per share. It tells investors how much cash we're actually generating from our regular business activities. Cash flow is super important for us as business owners because it's the lifeblood of our operations. It helps us cover expenses, invest in growth, and handle any unforeseen challenges that may come our way.

The price-to-cash flow ratio (P/CF) is a financial metric used to evaluate the relative value of a company's stock compared to its operating cash flow. It is similar to the more common price-to-earnings (P/E) ratio, but instead of using earnings, it uses cash flow as the denominator.

The formula for calculating the price-to-cash flow ratio is:

P/CF = Market Price per Share / Operating Cash Flow per Share

Where:

- Market Price per Share is the current stock price of the company.
- Operating Cash Flow per Share is the total operating cash flow generated by the company divided by the number of outstanding shares.

A low P/CF ratio suggests that the stock may be undervalued, as investors are paying less for each unit of cash flow generated by the company. Conversely, a high P/CF ratio may indicate that the stock is overvalued relative to its cash flow generation.

Now, let's dive into the strengths of the P/CF ratio. By focusing on cash flow, it shows us how much actual money the company is bringing in, which can be quite different from its reported earnings. Cash flow is critical for a company's day-to-day operations, investing in new projects, and paying off debts. A healthy cash flow means a company is better equipped to handle unexpected challenges or invest in future growth opportunities hence the **P/CF ratio is often seen as a more reliable metric because cash flow is harder to manipulate compared to earnings**. It gives investors a clearer picture of how well we manage our finances. So, a healthy P/CF ratio can be a positive signal to potential investors.

Let's compare the price-to-earnings ratio (P/E ratio) and the price-to-cash flow ratio (P/CF ratio) using a practical example to illustrate their differences and how they can provide different insights into a company's valuation.

Example Company: XYZ Ltd..

1. Price-to-Earnings Ratio (P/E ratio): Suppose the current market price of one share of XYZ Ltd.. is Rs. 50, and its earnings per share (EPS) is Rs. 2.50.

    P/E ratio = Market Price per Share / Earnings per Share (EPS)

    P/E ratio = Rs. 50 / Rs. 2.50

    P/E ratio = 20

    In this example, XYZ Ltd. has a P/E ratio of 20. This means investors are willing to pay 20 times the company's earnings per share to own one share of the company. A P/E ratio of 20 suggests that investors have relatively high expectations for XYZ Ltd.'s future earnings growth and are willing to pay a premium for its stock compared to its current earnings.

2. Price-to-Cash Flow Ratio (P/CF ratio): Let's assume that XYZ Ltd.'s operating cash flow per share is Rs. 4.00.

    P/CF ratio = Market Price per Share / Operating Cash Flow per Share

    P/CF ratio = Rs. 50 / Rs. 4.00

    P/CF ratio = 12.5

    In this example, XYZ Ltd. has a P/CF ratio of 12.5. This means investors are willing to pay 12.5 times the company's operating cash flow per share to own one share of the company. A P/CF ratio of 12.5 suggests that investors are placing a lower premium on the company's cash flow generation compared to its earnings.

Comparing the two ratios:

- P/E Ratio: 20
- P/CF Ratio: 12.5

In this practical example, the P/E ratio is higher than the P/CF ratio, indicating that investors have higher expectations for the company's earnings growth compared to its cash flow generation.

Interpretation:

- A high P/E ratio relative to the P/CF ratio can suggest that investors are optimistic about the company's growth potential, future profitability, or market position.
- A low P/E ratio relative to the P/CF ratio may indicate that investors have more conservative expectations about the company's earnings growth compared to its cash flow generation.

So, when we talk to investors or analyze our own company's performance, we need to keep these ratios in mind. Investors want to see that we have exciting growth prospects and can generate enough cash

It's important to note that both ratios have their strengths and limitations. The P/E ratio focuses on earnings, which can be influenced by accounting practices, while the P/CF ratio is based on cash flow, which provides a clearer picture of a company's ability to generate cash to fuel that growth. By understanding how investors view us through these ratios, we can better communicate our strengths and make our company more appealing to potential shareholders.

However, Investors need to go beyond these ratios and dig deeper into a company's financial statements, management team, competitive advantages, industry trends, and overall economic conditions along with cash flow. This holistic approach ensures a more informed investment decision.

In conclusion, as business owners, we should hold these financial ratios as valuable insights into how investors see us. The P/E ratio shows their expectations for our earnings potential, while the P/CF ratio highlights our ability to generate cash. By presenting a comprehensive view of our company, we can attract the right investors who understand and believe in our growth story. So, let's keep building a strong foundation for our business and make smart decisions that will lead to a successful future.

FREE CASH FLOW AND VALUATION

In this chapter, we'll delve into the topic of valuing a business. Before we begin, it's essential that we have accumulated knowledge from the entire book up to this point. This foundation of understanding will serve as a solid base for us to understand the intricacies of business valuation.

In the previous chapter, we gained insights into the investor's mindset during the valuation process. Now, our focus shifts towards valuing our very own business. Understanding how to evaluate our business is of paramount importance, especially when seeking to raise funds. We need to be aware of the aspects an investor might overlook or misunderstand while attempting to down the valuation.

This chapter will shed light on the valuation process, the different factors that play a role, and the reasons behind considering or excluding certain elements. Armed with this knowledge, we'll be well-prepared to confidently assess the value of our business. As a result, during fundraising discussions, we'll be able to identify any points an investor might be disregarding, leading to an undervaluation of our business. With this newfound understanding, let's sink into the topic and explore the various facets of business valuation.

Undoubtedly! Cash flow is super important when it comes to figuring out how much a business is really worth. cash flow tells us how much cash a business is bringing in and how much it's spending on a regular basis. It's not just about profit on paper; it's about real money coming in and going out.

For example, let's say this bakery made ₹100,000 in sales last year. But what if they had to spend ₹90,000 on ingredients, rent, staff salaries, and other expenses? In the end, they only have ₹10,000 left in their pocket. That's their cash flow - the money they can actually use for things like expanding the business, paying off loans, or rewarding investors.

Now, imagine another bakery that made ₹80,000 in sales but managed their expenses really well and only spent ₹60,000. In this case, they have ₹20,000 left over in cash flow. So, even though the first bakery had higher sales, the second one might be more valuable because it's generating more cash that can be reinvested or given back to investors.

When people value businesses, they often use cash flow as a key factor. It helps them see the real financial health of the company and whether it's a smart investment. If a business has strong positive cash flow, it's a good sign that it's running efficiently and has the potential to grow. On the other hand, if a business has negative cash flow, it might be a red flag. It means they're spending more money than they're making, and that could lead to financial troubles down the road. So, whether you're buying a business, investing in stocks, or just curious about a company's financial health, always pay attention to its cash flow. It gives you a clearer picture of how well the business is doing and how much it's really worth in the long run.

small business owners, there are various ways to figure out how much their business is worth. They might need to do this to get funding from external sources like banks or investors. These lenders and investors want to know the company's value based on the cash it generates from its day-to-day operations. Also, if business owners plan to sell their company, they'll need to know its value before putting it up for sale.

Selling a business is a big deal and requires a lot of planning, similar to when you first started your business. So, knowing its true value is crucial. It helps the owners understand what their hard work and efforts have built, and it helps potential buyers see what they'd be getting if they purchase the business.

To make this valuation process easier and more accurate, there are different methods available. It's essential to use the right approach that suits the specific type of business and the industry it operates in. so, The DCF method is the most widely used and internationally accepted method for business valuation. DCF stands for Discounted Cash Flow, and it's considered one of the most reliable ways to determine a company's worth.

Because it takes into account the company's expected cash flows over time and factors in the time value of money, the DCF method is highly regarded in the business and financial world. It's used by investors, analysts, and companies to make well-informed decisions about investments, mergers, acquisitions, and even fundraising. By relying on the DCF method, businesses and investors can better understand the real value of a company, making it a popular and trusted approach in the global financial landscape.

When conducting a Discounted Cash Flow (DCF) valuation, several important factors need to be carefully considered to arrive at an accurate and meaningful valuation. These factors include:

- **Free Cash Flow Projections**
- **Discount Rate (Cost of Capital)**
- **Terminal Growth Rate**
- **Terminal Value**
- **Sensitivity Analysis**

We will analysis, each point carefully with examples:

9.1   Free Cash flow

Free cash flow (FCF) is a financial metric that represents the amount of cash generated by a company's operations that is available for distribution to its investors and for potential investments in the business. It is a crucial indicator of a company's financial health and its ability to generate cash after accounting for all the necessary capital expenditures required to maintain and expand its operations.

The source of free cash flow, whether viewed from the company's perspective or the equity holder's perspective, begins with the company's operating performance after accounting for expenses and taxes. Starting with the company's bottom line, which is the Profit After Taxes (PAT), is an essential step in determining the true 'Free cash flow.'

By 'true' free cash flow, we mean identifying and considering all the non-cash expenses that were deducted from the company's profit while calculating net income (PAT) and adding them back. These non-cash expenses, such as depreciation and amortization, are accounting entries that reduce net income but do not involve any actual cash outflow. the true free cash flow is a crucial step in understanding the company's cash-generating capacity and its potential for growth and value creation.

There are two main types of free cash flow commonly used in financial analysis:

1. **Unlevered Free Cash Flow (UFCF)**: Unlevered free cash flow, also known as **"free cash flow to the firm"** (FCFF), represents the cash available to all investors (both equity and debt holders) of a company. It measures the cash generated by a company's operations before accounting for the effects of interest expenses and tax payments.

   Formula for Unlevered Free Cash Flow:

   UFCF = PAT + Interest*(1 - Tax Rate) + Non Cash Expenses - Capital Expenditures - Change in Net Working Capital

   Where:

   PAT = The company's net profit after tax

   Tax Rate = The company's effective tax rate

   Non cash Expenses = Non-cash expenses Like depreciation and amortization

   Change in Net Working Capital = The difference between the current and previous periods' net working capital (current assets minus current liabilities)

   UFCF is useful for assessing the overall cash-generating capability of a company and its ability to service both equity and debt holders.

2. **Levered Free Cash Flow (LFCF)**: Levered free cash flow, also known as "**free cash flow to equity**" (FCFE), represents the cash available to the company's equity shareholders after accounting for all expenses, interest payments on debt, and tax obligations.

    Formula for Levered Free Cash Flow:

    LFCF = Net Income + Non Cash Expenses - Capital Expenditures - Change in Net Working Capital + Borrowings

    Where:

    Net Income = The company's net profit after tax

    Debt Ratio = debt in the company

    Hence FCFF and FCFE are related to each other as follows:

    FCFE = FCFF – Interests(1 – Tax rate) + Net borrowing.

    Levered free cash flow is particularly relevant to equity investors because it shows how much cash is available to be distributed to shareholders through dividends, stock buybacks, or other equity-related activities.

It's essential to consider both types of free cash flow depending on the specific analysis and stakeholders involved. UFCF is more suitable for evaluating the company's overall financial health and enterprise value, while LFCF provides insights into the cash flow available to shareholders specifically.

We are creating one fictional illustration to understand FCFF and FCFE:

9.2 Illustration: ABC Manufacturing

Assumptions:

- Revenue: ₹1,000,000
- Cost of Goods Sold (COGS): ₹600,000
- Operating Expenses: ₹250,000
- Depreciation & Amortization: ₹50,000
- Interest Expenses: ₹20,000
- Tax Rate: 25%
- Capital Expenditures (CapEx): ₹100,000
- Change in Net Working Capital (NWC): ₹10,000
- Total Debt: ₹300,000
- Number of Shares Outstanding: 100,000

Step 1: Calculate FCFF

1. Net Income (PAT) = EBIT - Interest Expenses - Taxes
2. Net Income = ₹100,000 - ₹20,000 - ₹20,000 = ₹60,000
3. FCFF = Net Income + Interest*(1 - Tax Rate) + Depreciation & Amortization - CapEx - Change in NWC
4. FCFF = ₹60,000 +20000(1-.25) + ₹50,000 - ₹100,000 - ₹10,000 = ₹15,000

Step 2: Calculate FCFE

1. Interest Expenses after taxes = ₹15,000
2. Net Borrowing (Debt Issued - Debt Repaid) = Total Debt - Previous Year's Debt Net Borrowing = ₹300,000 - ₹0 = ₹300,000
3. FCFE = Net Income + Non Cash Expenses - Capital Expenditures - Change in Net Working Capital + Borrowings
4. FCFE = ₹60,000 + ₹50,000 - ₹100,000 - ₹10,000 + ₹ 300,000 = ₹ 300,000

Step 3: Calculate FCFE from 2nd formula

1.   FCFE = FCFF – Interests(1 – Tax rate) + Net borrowing.

2.   FCFE = ₹15,000 - ₹15,000+ ₹ 300,000 = ₹ 300,000

9.3   Discount rate (Cost of Capital)

Discount Rate is referred to as the "Cost of Capital." The cost of capital is a critical financial metric used by businesses to evaluate the profitability of potential investments or projects. It represents the rate of return required by investors or creditors to provide funds or capital to a company.

The cost of capital takes into account the cost of both debt and equity financing. For businesses, it's essential to understand the cost of capital because it helps determine whether a project or investment will generate returns higher than the cost of obtaining the capital.

Companies often calculate their cost of capital based on the weighted average cost of debt and equity, taking into consideration the interest rates on debt, the expected returns on equity, and the proportion of debt and equity in their capital structure. By comparing the cost of capital to the potential returns of an investment, companies can make informed decisions and ensure that the investments they undertake are economically viable and profitable.

In simpler terms, the cost of capital tells a company how much it needs to pay its investors or creditors for using their money to finance operations or growth initiatives. It's an important factor in decision-making and financial planning, helping businesses assess the feasibility of various investment opportunities and optimize their capital structure.

The cost of capital can be calculated using the Weighted Average Cost of Capital (WACC) formula. The WACC takes into account the cost of debt and the cost of equity, considering the proportion of debt and equity in the company's capital structure.

The formula for calculating the Weighted Average Cost of Capital (WACC) is as follows:

$$WACC = E/V \times re + D/V \times rd \times (1 - Tc)$$

Where:

- E = Market value of equity
- D = Market value of debt
- V = Total market value of equity and debt ($V = E + D$)
- re = Cost of equity (required rate of return on equity)
- rd = Cost of debt (required rate of return on debt)
- Tc = Corporate tax rate

Let's illustrate the calculation of the WACC with an example:

Example: ABC Manufacturing is a company with a capital structure consisting of 70% equity and 30% debt. The cost of equity is estimated at 12%, the cost of debt is 6%, and the corporate tax rate is 25%.

Market value of equity (E) = ₹700,000

Market value of debt (D) = ₹300,000

Total market value (V) = E + D = ₹700,000 + ₹300,000 = ₹1,000,000

Using the formula, we can calculate the WACC:

$$WACC = E/V \times re + D/V \times rd \times (1 - Tc)$$

WACC=700,000/1,000,000×0.12+300,000/1,000,000×0.06×(1−0.25)

WACC=0.07+0.015×0.75

WACC=0.07+0.01125

WACC=0.08125

In this example, the Weighted Average Cost of Capital (WACC) for ABC Manufacturing is 8.125%. This means that the company needs to earn a return of at least 8.125% on its investments to satisfy both its equity shareholders and debt holders.

The WACC is a critical metric for businesses as it helps in evaluating potential investment opportunities and guiding financial decisions. If a new investment or project has a return higher than the WACC, it is considered economically viable and can create value for the company and its shareholders

9.4 Terminal Growth Rate

The terminal growth rate, also known as the **perpetual growth rate**, is a crucial component used in financial valuation models, particularly in the context of discounted cash flow (DCF) analysis. It represents the expected long-term growth rate at which a company's cash flows, earnings, or dividends are assumed to grow indefinitely into the future.

In a DCF analysis, the terminal growth rate is used to estimate the cash flows beyond the explicit forecast period, which typically extends for a few years. Since it is not practical to forecast cash flows indefinitely, analysts use the terminal growth rate to assume a stable and sustainable growth rate for the company beyond the explicit forecast period.

Let's consider a fictional company called XYZ Ltd. that is expected to grow its free cash flows steadily over the next five years. After these five years, it may not be practical to forecast the cash flows in detail. Terminal growth assumes that XYZ Ltd. will keep growing, but at a stable rate beyond the five-year forecast period.

The terminal growth rate is influenced by various factors, including industry trends, economic conditions, market potential, and the company's competitive position. Analysts typically aim to choose a terminal growth rate that is in line with the expected long-term growth rate of the overall economy and industry.

It is important to use a reasonable and justifiable terminal growth rate in DCF analysis, as a high or unrealistic growth rate can lead to overvaluing a company, while an overly conservative rate may undervalue it. Terminal growth rate assumptions should be based on thorough analysis and consideration of the company's fundamentals and industry outlook.

Overall, the terminal growth rate plays a critical role in estimating the long-term value of a company and is a key factor in determining its intrinsic worth in financial valuation.

9.5 Terminal Value

Terminal value, also known as **perpetuity value or continuing value**, is a financial concept used in valuation to estimate the present value of all future cash flows of a company beyond a specific forecast period. Since it is impractical to forecast cash flows indefinitely, the terminal value represents the value of a company's cash flows that are expected to continue indefinitely into the future at a steady and sustainable growth rate.

In simple terms, the terminal value allows us to consider the long-term growth potential of a business beyond the period covered by detailed financial projections. It is particularly important in methods like the discounted cash flow (DCF) analysis, which aims to determine the intrinsic value of a company based on its expected future cash flows.

Suppose you forecasted your Coffee Shop's sales for the next five years, but you want to estimate its worth beyond that period. You'd use the terminal value to represent the total value of your Coffee Shop's future sales beyond the five years. This way, you don't miss out on considering its long-term potential.

The terminal value is calculated using the terminal growth rate (a reasonable assumption of the company's long-term growth rate) and the weighted average cost of capital (WACC) - the rate of return expected by investors. The formula for terminal value in a DCF analysis is:

$$\text{Terminal Value} = FCF_{n+1}/(WACC - g)$$

Where:

- FCF_{n+1} represents the expected free cash flow of the company in the year immediately following the forecast period.
- WACC is the weighted average cost of capital, which considers both the cost of debt and equity.
- g is the terminal growth rate, representing the assumed sustainable growth rate of the company.

Terminal value plays a critical role in estimating the overall value of a company, as it accounts for the cash flows expected beyond the explicit forecast period. In many cases, the terminal value constitutes a significant portion of the total company valuation. Therefore, accurate estimation of the terminal growth rate and careful consideration of factors affecting the company's long-term prospects are essential to arrive at a reliable valuation.

Ultimately, terminal value allows investors and analysts to take a comprehensive view of a company's financial prospects and make informed investment decisions based on its future growth potential.

9.6 Sensitivity Analysis

Sensitivity analysis is a powerful technique used in financial modeling and decision-making to assess the impact of changes in key variables on the outcome of a given model or analysis. It helps in understanding how sensitive the results are to variations in certain inputs, allowing decision-makers to identify which factors have the most significant influence on the outcomes.

In simple terms, sensitivity analysis helps answer questions like:

- How does a change in sales volume affect the company's profitability?
- What happens to the project's net present value if interest rates fluctuate?
- How sensitive is the valuation of a company to changes in growth rate assumptions?

Let's consider a real estate developer planning to construct a new commercial building. The developer creates a financial model to forecast the project's cash flows over the next ten years, taking into account variables like construction costs, rental income, operating expenses, and sales prices.

Using sensitivity analysis, the developer can test how variations in key factors impact the project's feasibility and profitability. For instance:

- They might change the rental income assumptions to see how different rent levels affect the project's net present value (NPV).
- They can also alter the construction cost estimates to assess how cost overruns impact the return on investment (ROI).
- By adjusting the sales price assumptions, they can evaluate the sensitivity of the project's payback period.

Sensitivity analysis provides valuable insights into the risk and uncertainty associated with a particular project or financial model. By understanding the sensitivities, decision-makers can make informed choices, identify potential risks, and develop contingency plans to mitigate adverse outcomes.

It's important to note that sensitivity analysis does not predict future outcomes with certainty; rather, it helps in making more informed decisions by exploring the range of potential outcomes based on different assumptions.

Overall, sensitivity analysis is a valuable tool that empowers businesses and investors to evaluate the robustness of their financial models, consider various scenarios, and make well-informed decisions in an ever-changing and uncertain environment.

9.7 Detailed Valuation Illustration

After Understanding on Free Cash Flow (FCF) projections, Discount Rate (Cost of Capital), Terminal Growth Rate, Terminal Value, and Sensitivity Analysis.

let's create a valuation illustration for a fictional company called "TechCo Inc.

Particulars	No. of Shares	Issue price	Amount
Share Capital	100000	10	1000000
Loans			500000
Cash and cash equivlant			400000
Cost of capital	12%		
Cost of debt	10%		
Tax rate	25%		
Terminal Growth	3%		

Particulars	Year 1	Year 2	Year 3	Year 4	Year 5
PAT	100,000	120,000	150,000	190,000	240,000
Depreciation	15,000	20,000	25,000	30,000	35,000
Interest	50,000	50,000	50,000	50,000	50,000
Changes in W.cap	36,000	42,000	45,000	52,000	60,000
Capex	50,000	50,000	50,000	50,000	50,000

Lets Calculate Fair Value per Share

Step 1:WACC

Cost of Equity Calculation		
Particulars	Rate	
Cost of Equity	12.0%	

Cost of Debt Calculation					
Particulars	Rate				
Cost of debt	10.00%				
Tax adjusted	7.50%				

WACC Calculation					
Particulars	Year 1	Year 2	Year 3	Year 4	Year 5
Debt	500,000	500,000	500,000	500,000	500,000
Shareholder Funds	1,100,000	1,220,000	1,370,000	1,560,000	1,800,000
Debt%	31.25%	29.07%	26.74%	24.27%	21.74%
Equity%	68.75%	70.93%	73.26%	75.73%	78.26%
Cost of Debt (Tax Adjusted)	7.50%	7.50%	7.50%	7.50%	7.50%
Cost of Equity	12.00%	12.00%	12.00%	12.00%	12.00%
Weighted Average Cost of Capital	10.59%	10.69%	10.80%	10.91%	11.02%
Average Weighted Average Cost of Capital	10.80%				

Step 2: Calculation for valuation

						(Amount in Rs.)
Particulars	Year 1	Year 2	Year 3	Year 4	Year 5	Terminal Value
PAT	100,000	120,000	150,000	190,000	240,000	
Add: Depreciation	15,000	20,000	25,000	30,000	35,000	
Add: Interest	50,000	50,000	50,000	50,000	50,000	
Less: Changes in W.cap	(36,000)	(42,000)	(45,000)	(52,000)	(60,000)	
Less: Capex	(50,000)	(50,000)	(50,000)	(50,000)	(50,000)	
Free cash flow	79,000	98,000	130,000	168,000	215,000	2,838,236
Timing Factor	1	2	3	4	5	5

					(Amount in Rs.)
Discounting Factor	0.90	0.81	0.74	0.66	0.60	0.60
Present Value (PV)	71,298	79,823	95,564	111,458	128,734	1,699,429

			Calculation of Terminal Value	
Enterprise value (Total of PVs)	2,186,307		**Calculation of Terminal Value**	
			$TV=(FCFn \times (1+g))/(WACC-g)$	2,838,236
Less: Loans	(500,000)		Where:	
Add: Cash and cash equivlant	400,000		FCFn = free cash flow of final year	215,000
			g = Terminal growth rate of FCF	3.00%
Present Value of Company for shareholders	2,086,307		WACC = weighted average cost of capital	10.80%
No. of Shares	100,000			
Value per Share (Rs.)	20.86			

Step 3: Senstivity Analysis

	WACC				
Terminal Growth	8.80%	9.80%	10.80%	11.80%	12.80%
2.00%	25.32	21.63	18.79	16.53	14.71
2.50%	27.11	22.92	19.76	17.29	15.30
3.00%	29.20	24.41	**20.86**	18.13	15.96
3.50%	31.70	26.14	22.11	19.07	16.69
4.00%	34.71	28.16	23.55	20.13	17.50

The table represents a sensitivity analysis for a company's valuation using different discount rates (Cost of Capital) and terminal growth rates. The values in the table show the estimated valuations of the company under various scenarios.

Here's how to interpret the table:

- The first column displays different terminal growth rates, ranging from 2.00% to 4.00%.
- The first row shows different discount rates, starting from 8.80% and increasing in increments of 1.00% to 12.80%.
- Each cell in the table represents the estimated valuation of the company for a specific combination of the discount rate and terminal growth rate.

For example, let's take the value in the cell where the discount rate is 10.80% and the terminal growth rate is 3.00%. The valuation of the company under this scenario would be ₹20.86.

If Discount rate reduced by 1 then the discount rate is 9.80% and the terminal growth rate is 3.00%. The valuation of the company under this scenario would be ₹24.41.That means if investor required rate of return is reduced by 1% then per share value jumped to Rs. 24.41 (if all other factor remain same)

Sensitivity analysis helps decision-makers assess how changes in critical variables impact the company's valuation. It shows how the valuation varies based on different assumptions, providing valuable insights into the company's financial risk and uncertainty.

In this table, you can observe that as the discount rate increases or the terminal growth rate decreases, the valuations generally decline i.e Rs. 14.71. Conversely, as the discount rate decreases or the terminal growth rate increases, the valuations tend to increase to Rs. 34.71.

The sensitivity analysis assists in making informed decisions by understanding how sensitive the company's valuation is to changes in the underlying assumptions. It also helps identify the critical factors driving the valuation, enabling decision-makers to develop appropriate strategies and contingency plans.

Keep in mind that this is just a hypothetical example, and real-world valuations involve a more comprehensive analysis of various factors and market conditions. The sensitivity analysis serves as a valuable tool for financial modeling and risk assessment, providing a clearer picture of the potential outcomes under different scenarios.

The cash flow statement is a vital tool for business owners to manage their companies effectively. Mastering this Cash flow helps avoid financial troubles and make informed decisions. It provides real-time insights, aids in planning, and identifies cash flow patterns. Creating and reviewing the cash flow statement becomes a lifelong report guiding business owners through their financial journey, ensuring resilience and success. "Hold its power and stay on track towards prosperity".